ALASKA'S HIDDEN WARS

# Alaska's Hidden Wars

## *Secret Campaigns on the North Pacific Rim*

### *Otis Hays, Jr.*

UNIVERSITY OF ALASKA PRESS, FAIRBANKS

*For information, contact:*
104 Eielson Building
P.O. Box 756240
Fairbanks, AK 99775-6240
(888) 252-6657
(907) 474-5831
fypress@uaf.edu
www.uaf.edu/uapress


Book design by Rachel Fudge
Cover design by Lisa Tremaine

Cover: Detail of a propaganda leaflet highlighting Attu Island; author's collection.


Printed in the United States of America.
This paper meets the requirements of ANSI/NISO Z39.48-1992 (Permanence of Paper).

LIBRARY OF CONGRESS CATALOGING-IN-PUBLICATION DATA
Hays, Otis.
Alaska's hidden wars : secret campaigns on the North Pacific rim / Otis Hays, Jr.
p. cm.
ISBN 1-889963-63-1 (alk. paper) — ISBN 1-889963-64-X (pbk. : alk. paper)
1. World War, 1939–1945—Campaigns—Alaska—Aleutian Islands. 2. World War,
1939–1945—Campaigns—Russia—Kuril Islands. 3. Aleutian Islands (Alaska)—History,
Military. 4. Kuril Islands (Russia)—History, Military. I. Title.
D769.87.A4H36 2004
940.54'28—dc22                                              2003020076

*For the Americans and Japanese who served in the North Pacific.*

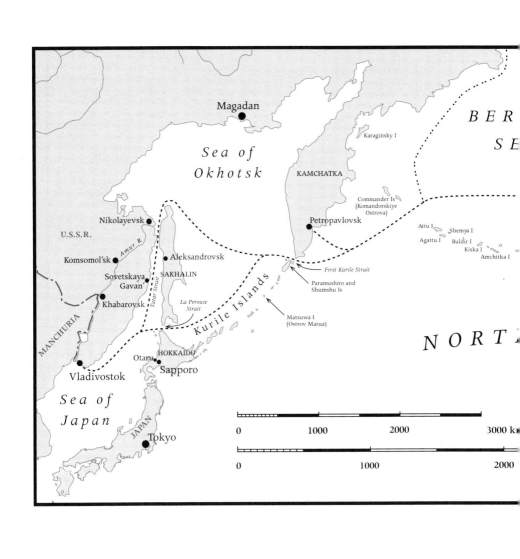

Magadan

*Sea of Okhotsk*

Karaginsky I

KAMCHATKA

*B E R*

*S E*

Commander Is
(Komandorskiye
Ostrova)

Nikolayevsk

U.S.S.R.

Petropavlovsk

Attu I

Shemya I

Agattu I    Buldir I

Kiska I

Amchitka I

Komsomol'sk

*Amur R*

Aleksandrovsk

SAKHALIN

First Kurile Strait

Paramushiro and
Shumshu Is

Sovetskaya
Gavan'

*Tatar Strait*

Khabarovsk

*La Perouse
Strait*

*K u r i l e   I s l a n d s*

Matsuwa I
(Ostrov Matua)

*N O R T*

MANCHURIA

Otaru

HOKKAIDO

Sapporo

Vladivostok

*Sea of
Japan*

JAPAN

Tokyo

| 0 | | 1000 | | 2000 | | 3000 k |
|---|---|---|---|---|---|---|

| 0 | | 1000 | | 2000 |
|---|---|---|---|---|

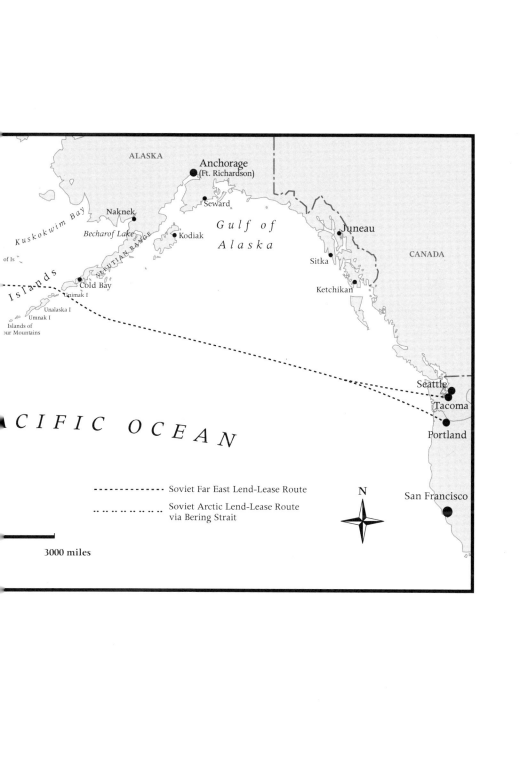

# Contents

# Illustrations

# Preface

**A**FTER **JAPAN ENTERED WORLD WAR II** in December 1941, the national interests of Japan, the United States, and the Soviet Union began to focus on the remote northwest corner of the Pacific Ocean. Japan's Kurile Islands chain extended from Hokkaido northeastward to the key anchor islands of Paramushiro and Shumushu. Cape Lopatka, on the southern tip of the Soviet Union's Kamchatka Peninsula, was visible from Shumushu. Only the narrow First Kurile Strait separated them. Nearly 800 miles to the east, Attu stood at the end of Alaska's Aleutian Islands chain.

The Kuriles, the Aleutians, and Kamchatka were volcanic and bleak. They were set amidst or bordered on frigid bodies of water where the Pacific Ocean, the Bering Sea, and the Sea of Okhotsk collided. The subarctic weather was notorious for its heavy fogs and fierce winds regardless of season. The weather rarely looked kindly on the conduct of military operations (see Chapter 8).

In the six months between the Pearl Harbor attack and the battle for Midway, Japanese strategists realized that, if the war were not quickly won, the northern Aleutian Islands–Kurile Islands route would be one of three likely avenues of enemy approach to the Japanese homeland. Therefore, in order to divert attention from their planned assault on Midway in early June 1942, the Japanese strategists also planned to make a surprise raid on the American Aleutian outpost at Dutch Harbor. Japanese transports then would land troops on Attu and Kiska in the outer Aleutians. The purpose of the islands' occupation was to neutralize or delay the American use of the northern islands' approach route to Japan.[1]

In the three war years that followed, an American two-phase military offensive ensued. The first phase was referred to as the "Aleutian campaign" of 1942–1943. The second phase later became known as a "forgotten war" or a "silent war" of 1943–1945. Both phases were executed behind an elaborate security curtain. In retrospect, both phases best could be called "hidden wars."

Historians have noted the June 1942 Japanese attack on Dutch Harbor and, a year later, the Japanese sacrificial defense to Attu and the undetected escape from Kiska. For most historians and the American public, however, the "real" war in the North Pacific ended on August 15, 1943, with the unopposed landing of Allied forces on abandoned Kiska.

Even before the Japanese abandoned Kiska, American planners prepared to change the direction of the military action in the North Pacific. The first air raids on the Kurile Islands were already introducing the American threat designed to heighten Japanese anxiety. Until recently, the Japanese had been defenders of occupied Attu and Kiska. Now, they were still defenders, but defenders of their own Kurile Islands outposts.

The author, a military intelligence officer in Alaska during World War II, was cognizant of many of the activities that were either concealed or denied during the hidden wars. For undisclosed historical information, he sought the classified Alaska Defense Command/Alaskan Department weekly military intelligence (G-2) reports of 1943–1945. He eventually located them in 1992 among the records of the National Archives, College Park, Maryland.[2]

Other clues to pertinent information came from the Naval Historical Center, Washington, D.C., and from the Air Force Historical Research Center, Maxwell Air Force Base, Alabama.

In addition, reminiscences, contributions, and photographs were furnished by Walter Bailey (deceased), Dallas, North Carolina; Mitchell Barchuk, DeBery, Florida; William Cavanaugh, Ocala, Florida; D. A. Cruse, Arlington, Virginia; Barbara Evison, Valley Center, California; Edward Fortier and Sylvania Kobayashi, both of

Anchorage, Alaska; Nobuo Furuiye, Denver, Colorado; Frank Imon, Las Vegas, Nevada; Juetts Kariya, Montebello, California; Col. Young O. Kim, Chikara Don Oka, and Akiko and Steve Yogi (deceased), all of Los Angeles, California; Mary Louise McEowen, Indianapolis, Indiana; A. R. ("Bob") Miller, Rough and Ready, California; Pete Nakao, Arista, California; Col. Irving Payne, West Long Beach, New Jersey; Lawrence Reineke, Middletown, New York; Richard Salter, Corsicana, Texas; Michael Schneider, Washington, D.C.; Gary Shearer, Angwin, California; Hal T. Spiden, Kingsport, Tennessee; Laura Tatsuguchi-Davis, Sherman Oaks, California; William S. Webb, San Juan Capistrano, California; Walter M. Webb, Rome, New York; and Milton E. Zack, Randolph, Massachusetts.

# Introduction

**I**N THE SUMMER OF 1941, the United States awakened to realize that, with wars spreading abroad, the American dream of neutrality was evaporating. American troops were being rushed overseas, including those bound for the new Alaska Defense Command (ADC). The commander, Brig. Gen. Simon B. Buckner, Jr.,[1] was in the midst of developing an emergency strategy to defend southeast Alaska, Nome, Fairbanks, Seward, Anchorage, Kodiak, and Unalaska (Dutch Harbor).

On August 6, 1941, four months before Japan attacked Pearl Harbor, Lt. Gen. John L. DeWitt, commander of the Fourth Army[2] at San Francisco, wrote a letter to Ernest Gruening, governor of the Territory of Alaska.[3] In the letter, DeWitt outlined a new "publicity policy" for Alaska, which laid the foundation for the development of the coming wartime security curtain in the North Pacific (see Chapter 1).

DeWitt's letter explained that the War Department, the Navy Department, and the Thirteenth Naval District,[4] as well as DeWitt's Fourth Army, were in full accord with the new policy. "It was agreed," the general wrote, "that, until further notice, there is to be no publicity with reference to Army stations in Alaska, or to troop movements to and within Alaska; and no newspaper or magazine correspondent, radio commentator, or other publicity agent is to be given any special access to Alaskan military stations, or to be authorized to publish or broadcast any information concerning the defense establishment there."

His letter continued: "The editors and managers of the most important newspapers and all of the news syndicates on the Pacific Coast have reiterated their willingness to cooperate with the Army and Navy in carrying out this policy, and this fact has been fully explained to writers who came to me for authority to give publicity to the Alaska defense program." DeWitt asked for the governor's full cooperation to insure that information of military value regarding Alaska would not be made available for publication.

The policy, still in effect when December 7 came and went, was soon strengthened when Washington officials reacted to the sudden presence of war.

In a realistic sense, World War II in the North Pacific began on November 27, 1941. That was when the War Department warned General DeWitt that a collapse of Japanese-American diplomatic relations could be imminent. The warning was passed to General Buckner, who called a full military alert in Alaska on November 28.[5] Despite the alert, Alaska was stunned nine days later by the December 7 attack on Pearl Harbor. Beyond the southwestern horizon, an armed enemy of unknown size and intention now faced Alaska's newly arrived, ill-equipped, and scattered forces.

In the immediate wake of the Japanese raid on Pearl Harbor, Radio Tokyo hinted of attacks on Alaska.[6] Rumors became rampant. During the confusion and suspense, public imagination found potential spies and saboteurs hidden in various areas of Alaska.

Both military and civilian authorities incorrectly suspected the Japanese of having crucial knowledge of Alaska's defense weaknesses. For years, Japanese fishing craft and even small naval vessels were reported to have visited and surveyed the barren outer Aleutian Islands, especially Attu and Kiska. However, when the Japanese did decide to move against Alaska in early 1942, it soon became apparent that any Japanese knowledge of the area east of Attu and Kiska was not current.

The Japanese encountered the early North Pacific security curtain for the first time when they sent a carrier battle fleet to attack

Dutch Harbor in June 1942. The enemy intended for the air raid to be a surprise diversion during the battle for Midway Island. Instead, unexpected American aircraft waited for the Dutch Harbor raiders. The reverse surprise signaled the beginning of Japanese frustration in gauging the ability and speed of American military forces to operate in the North Pacific.

After withdrawing their battle fleet from the Dutch Harbor area on June 4, the Japanese landed occupation troops on Attu and Kiska as planned. The American enthusiasm over Japan's Midway Island defeat was somewhat dampened by the news that enemy troops had gained a foothold in the Aleutians. To remove the enemy from American soil, the Aleutian campaign was launched island by island to reach Attu and Kiska during the next fifteen months. Public information regarding the offensive was tightly controlled.

With the Aleutians again in American possession, public attention was shifted to other battlefronts beyond the North Pacific. However, the security curtain remained in place to screen American plans for future military operations and deception efforts aimed at the Japanese Kurile Islands defenders. The Japanese difficulty in penetrating the security curtain and separating fact from fiction in the North Pacific endured throughout World War II.

# The Aleutian Islands

★ ★ ★

## 1941–1943

*Chapter One*

# Lowering the Security Curtain

**O**N **DECEMBER 16,** President Roosevelt anticipated that Congress would quickly approve legislation authorizing him to create, among other things, an Office of Censorship. He pointed out that "all Americans abhor censorship, just as they abhor war. But the experience of this and all other nations has demonstrated that some censorship is essential in wartime." Since the United States was now at war, he added, "it is necessary to the national security that military information which might be of aid to the enemy be scrupulously withheld at the source."[1]

Two days later, on December 18, Congress passed the First War Powers Act. The president wasted no time. On the following day he issued an executive order creating the Office of Censorship. He named Byron Price, a nationally known newsman, as its director. Price realized that, although he was responsible solely to the White House, he was undertaking a thankless and distasteful task.[2]

Under Price's direction, a network of censorship examination stations was located on the nation's coastlines and borders. Here international mail, cable, radio, and telephone communications were monitored for content. If the content warranted, the communications were interrupted or seized.

No attempt was made to censor America's domestic print and broadcast media. Instead, at the request of the president, Price enlisted and obtained the cooperation of editors and publishers to censor themselves. On January 15, 1942, Price issued the guidelines for a Code of Wartime Practices for the American Press. In it, the press was cautioned against publishing material of interest and benefit to the enemy, such as information about shipping, aircraft, troops, fortifications, war production, and armaments, especially secret weapons. At the same time, a similar code was issued for American radio broadcasters. The major difference between the two codes was the omission or use of weather information. Radio broadcasters were asked not to mention weather conditions and forecasts because the enemy could intercept the information. On the other hand, publishers were permitted limited use of official weather reports.[3]

Adherence to the voluntary codes did not always produce desirable results. Nevertheless, publishers and radio station managers became aware that the nation's wartime security was also their patriotic business.

Although not identified as direct censorship, the official bureaucratic practice of delaying the release of war news stories accomplished the same goal. Details of major battles, especially the disclosure of American losses, were postponed until the Army and Navy were convinced that the knowledge would not benefit the enemy.[4]

The Army and Navy, not the Office of Censorship, were responsible for censoring the mail to and from their forces overseas—which included the military forces in the Territory of Alaska.

The Territory of Alaska was promptly designated a military combat area in which General Buckner's Alaska Defense Command had the authority and responsibility to commence military postal censorship. Army officers in unit command positions read and cleared the letters written by their men. Officers themselves certified by signature that their own letters did not violate censorship rules. However, censors at specified bases spot-checked the mail of men and officers. The Navy had a similar censorship system.[5]

To be effective, censorship was also applied to the mail of Alaskan civilians. The Office of Censorship's postal examination stations at Seattle and later at Minneapolis monitored the flow of civilian correspondence.

At the request of the Office of Censorship, the Army and Navy agreed to be responsible for the interception and examination of cable, radiotelegraph, and landline telephone communications to and from Alaska.[6]

The military censors were loaded down with regulations that covered not only questions of security but also broad matters of military policy.[7] Lacking the flexibility and experience to cope with the extraordinary wartime conditions, overzealous censors were faced with an upset Governor Gruening and furious independent-minded Alaskans, who commenced a storm of protest. The first year of the war would pass, however, before 150 trained military censors would arrive to oversee the censorship program.

Alaskan newspaper editors and radio station managers agreed to abide by the Office of Censorship's two codes of wartime practices.[8] Although the media's intentions were honest, their willingness to self-censor was rarely applicable because their access to military information was limited. Since Alaska was a designated military combat area, news items of military importance were rigidly controlled by military public relations officers.

The Code of Wartime Practices did not apply to war correspondents. Instead, overseas military commanders, including General Buckner, allowed officially accredited correspondents to accompany combat units if the newsmen agreed to submit their reports and photographs to military public relations officers for clearance.[9]

**ONE OF THE EARLY SECURITY CURTAIN RESTRICTIONS** in Alaska was aimed at resident Japanese-Americans. Special attention was immediately directed to Harry Sotaro Kawabe, a successful and well-known

Seward businessman. The war was only hours old when military authorities ordered his detention.

At the end of the nineteenth century, the continental West Coast's predominantly Caucasian population had yet fully to accept the presence of immigrant Japanese issei (first generation). American-born nisei (second generation), even though they were American citizens, also faced social and economic discrimination because of their Japanese parentage.

Only a handful of Japanese issei were Alaskan residents. Harry Sotaro Kawabe was one of them. An ambitious immigrant, Kawabe arrived in Seattle in 1906. Learning of the opportunities and higher wages in Alaska, he moved there and eventually settled in Seward.[10] Strategically located at the head of Resurrection Bay, Seward was the ocean terminal for the Alaska Railroad and the port of entry for supplies bound for the Alaska mainland. Having arrived via ship at Seward, the cargoes were moved by the railroad into interior Alaska as far as Fairbanks. Seward's maritime-railroad connection with the West Coast was considered critical to the early defense of Alaska.[11]

After establishing himself at Seward in 1915, Kawabe quickly gained prosperity and prominence. He invested in and expanded numerous real-estate and business enterprises, including the Seward Laundry. He soon was considered not only an outstanding business-man but the foremost Japanese-American in Alaska as well. Although he was active in community affairs and generously sup-ported children's education, Kawabe attracted the attention of sus-picious governmental and military investigators. Among other items, the investigators reported that (1) officers of the Imperial Japanese Navy had contacted Kawabe in 1935, (2) over a period of years he helped numerous Japanese nationals visit Alaska, and (3) he had been instrumental in arranging the shipment of scrap iron from Alaska to Japan. Later, documents found in his possession were alleged to have been issued by Japanese military and naval officers.[12]

Reacting immediately to Japan's raid on Pearl Harbor, the Alaska Defense Command ordered Kawabe to be detained on the evening of December 7. Kawabe was waiting with his wife in their apartment on the upper floor of his laundry building. Because of the hysterical anti-Japanese rumors that already were spreading through town, Kawabe was moved quickly to the railroad station and smuggled under escort in a railroad freight train caboose to Anchorage. Two days later, Kawabe's four Japanese-American laundry employees, who resided with their families in Kawabe-owned apartments, were likewise smuggled to Anchorage for temporary detention. A month later, Kawabe's wife, Tomo, and the wives and children of Kawabe's employees joined the men.[13]

On the West Coast, public outcry against resident Japanese-Americans quickly reached Washington. The cries were so great that President Roosevelt signed Executive Order 9066 on February 19, 1942. The order authorized General DeWitt to relocate the 120,000 Japanese-Americans, issei and nisei alike, from his West Coast military zone to isolated inland camps. In the wake of General DeWitt's action, General Buckner also relocated Alaska's resident Japanese-Americans. On April 7, he ordered "all males of the Japanese race over nineteen years of age of half-blood" to report to the nearest military post by April 20 for relocation camps in the continental United States.[14]

Of the 263 Japanese-Americans who were relocated from Alaska, only eighty-eight were issei. Harry Kawabe became the Alaskan exiles' spokesman. In 1944 and 1945, some of them made petitions for release and return to their Alaskan homes. Some of the petitions were approved, but Kawabe, who petitioned twice, was denied.[15]

In addition, Buckner also ordered the evacuation of all military dependents from the Alaskan military combat area. Needless civilians in Alaska, he argued, would only complicate the maintenance and effectiveness of the security curtain.

With official high-level support, Buckner continued to ignore the resounding public protests, led by most of the Alaskan editors and

Governor Gruening himself, against censorship and mounting military restrictions. He soon would reaffirm and strengthen his security curtain policies to reduce the private and public flow of unauthorized or classified information from Alaska.

It was essential that the enemy not learn how vulnerable were the North Pacific defenses, especially at Dutch Harbor. Preparations were being made to cope with a Japanese attack of unknown size at an unknown time. In haste, the Army, with the cooperation of the Civil Aviation Administration, secretly built two emergency airfields, one on Umnak Island and the other at Cold Bay on the flanks of Dutch Harbor. The Navy concentrated its air and surface forces at Kodiak and Dutch Harbor. The only American outpost in the western Aleutians was a weather station on Kiska that the Navy was in the process of establishing (see Chapter 2).

*Chapter Two*

# Confrontation in the Aleutians

**F**OG, RAIN, WIND, EVEN SNOW AND ICE—the inhospitable Aleutian weather was a continuing challenge to any military activity across the North Pacific. The success of any future defense or offense would be dependent on reasonable knowledge of what to expect from the changing Aleutian atmospherics.

Immediately after the Pearl Harbor disaster, the Navy took emergency action to begin an assessment of current Aleutian weather conditions. On December 26, 1941, the Navy rushed a four-man cadre to Kiska Island with equipment and supplies to establish a weather station. Accompanying the men was their mascot, a black mongrel dog named Explosion.

Five months later, on May 19, 1942, six more men were sent to Kiska to reinforce the weather station complement. Aerographers Mate 1st Class W. C. House was in charge of the detachment.[1]

Later in May, the Commander-in-Chief, Pacific (CINCPAC), warned that a Japanese carrier force with troop transports was approaching the fog-bound Aleutians. On June 3 and 4, bombers from two enemy carriers twice found and pounded Dutch Harbor and its Unalaska environs. The persistent dismal weather and the surprising resistance by Navy and Army aircraft from the nearby secret bases convinced the carrier force to withdraw. However, the standby Japanese transports then prepared to land occupation troops on unprotected Attu and Kiska.

Among the American Dutch Harbor casualties were three Navy PBY airmen who became the first American prisoners of war in the North Pacific. They were captured from a life raft by the crew of the Japanese cruiser *Takao* after Japanese fighters shot down their Navy flying boat. Ensign Wylie M. Hunt, Seaman 1st Class Joseph R. Brown, and Aerographers Mate 3rd Class Carl Creamer successfully resisted interrogation. They were later delivered to a prisoner-of-war camp in Japan.[2]

Aerographers Mate House on Kiska, informed by radio of the Dutch Harbor raid, correctly foresaw that the Japanese would soon arrive. He and his men began hiding vital food supplies in Kiska's nearby ravines. Early on June 7, gunshots from a Japanese landing party awakened the weather detachment.

Aerographers Mate Winfrey, suffering from a leg wound, was the only casualty. However, he was able to flee with the other men through the fog into Kiska's interior. In a matter of days, the Japanese located nine of the ten weathermen and the hidden supplies. Only House evaded capture by hiding in the hills and caves. At first, House believed that the Japanese would destroy the weather station and then depart. He waited week after week. But instead of leaving, the Japanese landed more troops and prepared to remain indefinitely on the American island. Meanwhile, assuming that House was dead, the Japanese sent the nine captured weathermen by ship to Japan.

At the same time on June 7 that the Japanese troops were scattering the Navy weathermen on Kiska, other troops came ashore on Attu. The island's only inhabitants were forty-two Aleuts and two Caucasian employees of the Alaska Native Service, Etta Jones (teacher) and her husband, Foster Jones (radio operator), all residing in Chichagof Village. Foster Jones was the sole invasion casualty, who, it was believed, may have chosen suicide rather than submission to the enemy. Etta Jones was placed aboard a ship on June 15 and sent to Japan, where she joined a group of interned Australian nurses for the war's duration. On the same day, John Artumonoff's death of unknown cause reduced the number of Attu's Aleuts to forty-one.[3]

After Japanese troops landed on Attu and captured the villagers, American authorities feared that the Pribilof Islands of St. Paul and St. George and the Aleutian Island of Atka could be the enemy's next targets. As a result, Aleut villagers, carrying personal possessions, were evacuated from the vulnerable islands in mid-June. Later, Aleuts on Akutan, Umnak, and Unalaska were also evacuated. The Aleuts were relocated to remote camps in southeastern Alaska until the end of hostilities.[4]

Meanwhile, on Kiska, House managed to evade the enemy occupation forces for seven weeks by eating earthworms and vegetation. Finally, weakened and starving, he surrendered on July 26.

The Japanese at home were urged to celebrate the seizure of the American territory in the Aleutians as a major victory. The Japanese news agency Domei ordered its correspondent on Kiska, Mikizo Fukazawa, to interview House following his surrender. Fukazawa quoted House as saying, "I am grateful to the Japanese army for their kindness. I should have surrendered sooner."

Fukazawa wrote, "I felt sorry for him. As I listened to the man, I learned a lesson in the difference between Japanese and Americans."[5] It was unthinkable, Fukazawa wrote, for a Japanese soldier to be captured alive, because such an act would bring eternal disgrace to himself and his family. Fukazawa himself was not a soldier, but he was alluding to the traditional samurai military code of bushido (the way of the warrior). Victory or death was the choice given to Japanese men being indoctrinated for battle.

In August, the Japanese decided to abandon Attu in order to reinforce Kiska. Both the Japanese garrison and the Attu natives, bound for Kiska, evacuated Attu on September 17. During the short voyage, another Aleut, Anecia Prokopioff, died. On September 20, Navy weatherman W. C. House joined the remaining forty Aleuts aboard the *Nagata Maru* and sailed for Japan.[6]

During the first months of the war, the American armed forces were on the defensive throughout the Pacific. Tens of thousands of Americans, including many in the Philippines, became prisoners of war. In contrast, only a meager number of Japanese soldiers were taken alive. Five of them were captured in the Aleutians. In late August, the Japanese submarine *RO-61* found the Navy seaplane tender *Casco* in Atka Island's Nazan Bay and torpedoed it. Damaged but still afloat, the *Casco* was beached. Meanwhile, Navy PBY flying boats bombed the submarine and disabled it. The destroyer *Reid* located the damaged craft, forced it to the surface with depth charges, and then sank it. Five rescued Japanese crewmen were later sent to Hawaii for interrogation.[7] To their surprise, American interrogators found the Japanese prisoners willing to cooperate. Since there had been no anticipation that any Japanese would survive as prisoners of war, the men had not been schooled to resist interrogation. Therefore, disciplined to absolute obedience, the Japanese captives automatically obeyed their American interrogators and responded to their questions.[8]

The yearlong Aleutian campaign was now under way. While Navy warships scoured the seas west of Umnak, Army bombers began long-range harassment missions from Umnak's forward air base. Unfortunately, the missions were undertaken by pilots lacking current knowledge of the western Aleutian weather conditions that awaited at Kiska and Attu. As a result, bomber losses began to mount (see Chapter 8).

An Aleutian air base closer to the enemy-occupied islands was desperately needed. Although several islands were considered, Adak became General Buckner's choice in August.

While planning the seizure of Adak, Buckner continued his efforts to deny the enemy any hint of his Aleutian campaign by reinforcing his security curtain. Because civilians had long been free to enter Alaska by ship or plane, Buckner decided that the easy passage to and from Alaska must cease. Therefore, on June 30, less than a month after the enemy entered the Aleutians, Buckner

announced the establishment of Alaska Travel Control (ATC).[9]
Civilians desiring to enter or depart Alaska were required to obtain
travel permits. As in the case of censorship, the operation of ATC
was handicapped at first by inexperienced personnel and cumber-
some bureaucratic procedures, though in time the system became
more efficient.

In the immediate aftermath of the Japanese raid on Dutch Harbor,
Alaskan public attention was focused on the possible threat to the
Alaskan mainland itself. Like the earlier December shock when war
erupted, many Alaskans felt panic. Would or could Japanese forces
actually invade Alaska? After it was learned that the Japanese striking force instead had moved westward to occupy Kiska and Attu,
domestic tensions began to ease. In October, Buckner announced
that in August American forces had successfully landed and established an advance military base on Adak Island, about 400 miles
west of Dutch Harbor and only 250 miles from Kiska. Despite the
two-month delay in learning the news, many Alaskans assumed that
since American forces were counterattacking the Japanese, the
threat to mainland Alaska had virtually disappeared.[10]

Alaskans therefore anticipated that some of the military restrictions, especially ATC, would be modified or even lifted. They were
not. Buckner insisted that the security curtain was needed to screen
the conduct of the Aleutian campaign as American forces began to
leapfrog toward the end of the Aleutian Islands chain to remove all
Japanese presence from American territory. Looking beyond the
expulsion, Buckner also wanted to discourage any premature speculation concerning possible American plans to use the northern invasion route to Japan's homeland.

As the Aleutian campaign accelerated during the fall of 1942,
Buckner kept tight control of the flow of news and photographs by
limiting the number of accredited war correspondents in the combat
area. During the campaign, fewer than two dozen war correspondents were permitted in the Aleutians.[11] Although they applied,
local Alaskan newsmen were never accredited.[12]

Two of the correspondents, Howard Handleman and William Gilman, later wrote books about the experience. In his, Gilman criticized the motives of the security curtain. The effort to control news, he wrote, went beyond the usual boundaries because "it toyed dangerously with the psychological."[13]

John Huston, the motion picture producer/director, came to the Aleutians with his cameramen to make a propaganda film during the winter months. The cameramen rode with bomber crews as the Aleutian air war intensified. Censors withheld Huston's *Report from the Aleutians* until the campaign was over.[14]

Having won the race with the Japanese to occupy Adak, Buckner quickly established a new forward air base there. He joined the Navy in transferring their advance command posts (ACPs) from Kodiak to Adak.

Faced with the menacing new American air base on Adak, in October the Japanese reoccupied Attu and again reinforced the Kiska garrison. Both forces were girding for the decisive battle for possession of the Aleutians. American harassment of the Japanese on Attu and Kiska became unrelenting. When weather permitted, naval gunfire, bombs, and propaganda leaflets peppered both enemy-held islands. (A discussion and examples of propaganda leaflets are contained in Appendix B.)

Even though he had evacuated all Japanese-Americans from Alaska for security reasons, Buckner asked for and welcomed Army teams of fluent Japanese-language intelligence specialists—Japanese-American nisei—to support the Aleutian campaign. The nisei filled vital military-intelligence voids. Their secret presence and support in the Aleutians remained undisclosed, even though they served with troops in the Attu and Kiska operations (see Chapters 3 and 4).

*Chapter Three*

# The Secret Nisei in the Aleutian Campaign

**B**ECAUSE THE JAPANESE LANGUAGE was exceedingly difficult for foreigners to master, the Japanese government and military leaders mistakenly relied on that linguistic handicap to help in maintaining their documentary and communications security. They became lax. They never realized that one of the most important American secret military weapons in the Pacific war was the linguistic service of Japanese-American nisei. Nor was the American public cognizant of the secret until 1972. A quarter century after the war, the military records of nisei soldiers were declassified, revealing their unique skills and devotion to duty.

As military-intelligence language specialists, the nisei accompanied American combat units into every battle, translated hordes of otherwise unintelligible captured documents and intercepted messages, and interrogated Japanese prisoners as their number increased from a few to many in the closing months of the war. In addition to service with American forces in the island-by-island Pacific campaigns, including Attu and Kiska, they also assisted Allied forces of Canada, Great Britain, Australia, New Zealand, and China.

Despite the racial prejudice that existed among many of their fellow Americans, numerous nisei nevertheless volunteered for military service. Other nisei were recruited from the internment camps where they had been relocated with their parents and siblings.[1]

The early nisei volunteers attended Japanese-language refresher courses at the Fourth Army Intelligence School at the Presidio of San Francisco. The need for more Japanese-language specialists was quickly recognized. The teaching facility, renamed the Military Intelligence Service Language School, was later moved to Camp Savage and then to Fort Snelling, both in Minnesota.[2] A small, separate group of recruits, already proficient in the language, were the kibei, American offspring of issei who had been sent to Japan for education.

The volunteers and recruits were organized into Japanese-language Military Intelligence Service (MIS) teams. Each of the team members became a noncommissioned officer ranging variously from corporal to staff sergeant. Qualified Caucasian military-intelligence officers coordinated the MIS team activities in the combat areas.

In Alaska, General Buckner's intelligence staff developed the organizational framework for the employment of linguists. The Interpreters and Interrogators (I&I) Detachment contained two unrelated sections. One was for Russian-language interpreters necessary to conduct liaison functions with the future Soviet Military Mission personnel at Fairbanks and Nome. The other was for Japanese-language interrogators destined to engage in secret intelligence activities during the Aleutian campaign.[3]

On the eve of the Dutch Harbor raid, the first MIS team of five linguists arrived in Alaska and became the nucleus of the new I&I Japanese section. The team was promptly given the task of translating Japanese-language correspondence and documents from Harry Kawabe's office files in Seward.

A few weeks later, during the early stages of the Aleutian campaign, thirteen additional MIS graduates arrived to join the I&I organization. When the battles for Attu and Kiska were imminent, the arrival of additional nisei (Figure 2) then brought the I&I Japanese section to its full strength of forty Japanese-American linguists (Appendix A).

The first three officers for the section were Capt. John White, Lt. Gordon Jorgensen, and Lt. H. Sholty. Both White and Jorgensen were MIS-schooled graduates. Sholty had served his church in

Figure 2. Ten MIS nisei who helped bring the Alaska Defense Command's I&I Japanese-language section to strength for the Attu-Kiska campaign. *Front row* (left to right): **Mitsuru Shibata, Steve Yagi, Dick Oda, Chikara Don Oka.** *Back row:* **Ted Ishida, Harold Nishimura, Toshiro Sugimoto, Hiroma William Wada, George Muto.** The tenth man (not shown) was the photographer. Photo courtesy Chikara Don Oka.

Japan but volunteered his noncombatant services as a Japanese linguist after his return to the United States.

Meanwhile, in January 1943, Captain White introduced his first nisei to active service in the Aleutian campaign. Braving a vicious Aleutian storm, Army forces successfully island-hopped forward and landed on Amchitka (where an air base could bring the Kiska and Attu targets even closer). An Alaska Scout G-2 reconnaissance unit was in the vanguard of the landing force. Two I&I nisei— Yoshio Hotta and Masami Mayeda—accompanied the unit. A month later, White also sent Frank Imon and Shigeo Ito to Amchitka on temporary duty with the 102nd Signal Radio Intelligence Company's listening post, where they monitored Japanese voice radio transmissions (see Signal Intelligence Operations, Appendix D).

Following the American decision to bypass the Kiska stronghold in order first to eliminate the smaller enemy garrison on Attu, White ordered his I&I personnel, including those on Amchitka, to assemble at Adak. He assigned missions for each of his men to perform during the coming battle. A portion of the I&I section would remain at the Adak base to translate captured documents. The remainder would be available to support, directly or indirectly, the Seventh Infantry Division, which had been selected to regain American possession of Attu.[4]

White planned for highly qualified nisei, including Pete Nakao, to accompany the Seventh Division's assault forces on Attu. In mid-April, White and his selected team flew to Fort Ord, California. Here the Seventh Division, expecting to serve in North Africa, was completing its final desert warfare training. Because the unexplained appearance of the nisei at Fort Ord could arouse speculation, their presence was concealed. Days later, in late April, "the division was moved to Seattle where the infantrymen boarded waiting transports," Pete Nakao recalled. "When the transports were at sea, the men were told to exchange their desert combat outfits for Alaskan gear. For the first time, they realized that they were *not* going to Africa." No longer concealed, White and his nisei were also aboard the convoy bound for the Aleutians and the approaching battle for Attu.[5]

Twenty nisei were given Attu assignments but, as White planned, not all of them went ashore. Some of them were scattered aboard the nearby transports and warships. Two of them, Frank Otsuka and Mickey Kuroiwa, were stationed offshore throughout the battle to monitor Japanese radio traffic that might reveal any enemy decision and action to aid the Attu defenders. On two occasions during the lengthy battle, Japanese bombers from Paramushiro attempted to reach and strike American land and sea forces. Alerted American fighters met and routed them both times. The isolated Japanese on Attu were then abandoned to their fate.

*Chapter Four*

# Nisei Support at Attu and Kiska

**I** **N 1943, THE VIOLENT ISLAND FIGHTING** in the Pacific Ocean area produced the capture of 522 Japanese prisoners. Twenty-nine of them would be the sole Japanese survivors of the battle for Attu.[1]

In the beginning, the Japanese commander, Col. Yasuyo Yamasaki, anticipated the American landings on Attu and withdrew his estimated 2,900 army, navy, and civilian personnel from Attu's shores and moved them into the island's snow-covered mountains.[2] Here he prepared them to make a stubborn defense.

On May 11, despite fog, frigid temperatures, high winds, and heavy seas, the Seventh Division's superior force came ashore on two sides of Attu. The campaign, originally planned for victory in three days, would require six times that. The Seventh Division, reinforced by Alaska's Fourth Infantry Regiment, would finally locate, isolate, and defeat the outnumbered but elusive enemy.

Immediately following the landings, White moved his I&I section headquarters ashore. With him were Sam Sugimoto and Yasuo Sam Umetani. White had already assigned one or two nisei to accompany each major combat unit during the battle. They included Yashio Hotta, Hiroma William Wada, Tadashi Ogawa, Juetts Kariya, Satsuki Tanakatsubo, Pete Nakao, Howard Nakamura, Shigeo Ito, and Frank Imon (Figure 3). White realized that the nisei in the combat areas needed a measure of protection from fellow Caucasian soldiers, who

Figure 3. First assembled on Adak for the Attu-Kiska campaign were twelve I&I nisei and their officer. *Front row* (left to right): Henry Suyehiro, Shigeo Ito, Pete Nakao, Juetts Kariya, Hiroma William Wada. *Back row:* Hiroshi Kanagaki, Frank Imon, Howard Nakamura, George Hayashida, Lt. (later Capt.) Sholty, Yoshio Hotta, Ben Morikawi, Jake Kawakami. Photo courtesy Irving Payne, signal intelligence unit commander. Four of the above men were temporarily used as his radio intelligence monitors.

might mistake them for the enemy. He therefore insured that his I&I linguists were provided with Caucasian bodyguards.

George Hayashida went ashore with Gordon Jorgensen for special missions. Early in the battle, the two men astonished White by appearing without warning at White's command post. They had walked across the island through enemy-held territory, but were unscathed.

Pete Nakao was originally paired with Howard Nakamura to accompany the Thirty-second Infantry Regiment, but Nakamura became ill and was unable to land with Nakao. With his bodyguard, Harold Peterson, Nakao reached the unit's advance command post, where he remained throughout the battle.[3]

Having recovered, Nakamura later joined Satsuki Tanakatsubo. The destroyer that was responsible for landing them on the island was delayed when approaching Japanese bombers from Paramushiro were reported. For safety's sake, the destroyer was ordered to leave the area temporarily.

Frank Imon was attached to the Thirty-second Infantry Regiment's intelligence section. During lulls in the lengthy battle, he and other nisei made fake *hinomaru* Japanese battle flags. In exchange for the "genuine captured" Japanese flags offered to officers on naval vessels anchored offshore, Imon and his friends obtained fresh meat from the ships' stores.[4]

On May 26, while the Japanese defenders continued to endure the bloody fighting amidst the fog and snow, two lost, confused, and starving Japanese soldiers surrendered. Although the battle had raged for two weeks, they were the first to be captured. White's nisei interrogators found the two men ready to respond to their questions. Based on the prisoners' answers, it was clear that (1) the Japanese situation was one of desperation, (2) the Japanese artillery had been silenced, (3) the small-arms ammunition supply was approaching the point of zero, (4) food was so scarce that ration allowances had been cut repeatedly to a fraction of the men's daily need, and (5) any help from the Kurile Islands was no longer expected.

White reported the information to Gen. Eugene Landrum, the Seventh Division commander. The general decided to make an appeal to Colonel Yamasaki. Landrum ordered a surrender leaflet that offered Yamasaki an honorable way to end the useless battle.

Sam Sugimoto and White prepared the Japanese-language texts for several leaflets containing the central theme of an honorable cease-fire. On May 28, a low-flying plane scattered the leaflets over the area where Japanese troops were believed to be concentrated.[5]

Yamasaki was ready to respond, but not in the way that General Landrum had hoped for. In a plan born of desperation, Yamasaki sought an opportunity to break through the American lines in order to reach the Seventh Division supply dumps in Massacre Valley. With replenished food and ammunition, he hoped he then would be able to lead the remnants of his defense force back into the mountains and resume a battle of attrition.

Having first given Yamasaki an opportunity to surrender his remaining men, Landrum was ready for the final drive to complete the hard-earned American conquest of Attu. On the dark night of May 29–30, quiet reigned on the front. Because of the night's inactivity, a Thirty-second Infantry combat unit was allowed to retire to the rear for a hot meal before returning to its battle-rim position.

Yamasaki was now ready to execute his plan. With Japanese patrols leading the way, nearly a thousand men—all that remained of Yamasaki's defense force—found the gap in the lines and launched a screaming, bayonet-wielding banzai charge.

Pete Nakao and his bodyguard, Harold Peterson, were in the direct path of the oncoming Japanese at the Thirty-second Regiment's advance command post. He recalled the confusion and deaths in the melee that marked the final battle early on May 30:

That evening our front line outfit went past us and back [to the rear]. We thought that the outfit was being replaced with fresh troops. No way! We were all by ourselves at the command post. . . . It was pitch black when the enemy began the banzai attack. Harold and I were scrunched in one slit trench. All of a sudden, the enemy was upon us. We could not see anything in the darkness except for tracer bullets flying in every direction. Hoping to escape the jabbing bayonets, Harold and I stayed in our hole. Leaving bayonetted dead and wounded behind them, the Japanese went past us and continued to the medic unit station to our rear. Then they headed for the ammunition dump behind the medics.

By that time, our forces had rallied and surrounded the Japanese. During the confusion, Harold and I got separated. I found some of our anti-tank gunners who had been stationed at our command post. Some had been bayonetted next to their guns. I was passing out cigarettes to the [live] guys when Harold finally found me.

After daylight, our infantry surrounded the enemy right below our command post. From our vantage point, we could see the enemy huddled in one bunch. One guy stood up and said something to his men, and they squatted down and hand-grenaded themselves.

The battle won, Nakao and Peterson again became separated. During the remaining two years of the war, Nakao tried to locate Peterson but failed. They never saw each other again.[6]

Only a handful of Japanese survived the banzai charge and its aftermath. Yamasaki's body, sword in hand, was found where he fell. All of his officers also died. Most of the several hundred Japanese enlisted men who were not killed during the final charge preferred to die by their own hand.

Fourteen dazed Japanese, some of them wounded, were found among the broken bodies. The I&I nisei began to search the numerous caves for hidden men. A small group was located in the depths of one large cave. Speaking Japanese in an effort to calm the men, George Hayashida and Gordon Jorgensen, armed with flashlights and pistols, entered the cave and finally persuaded the ten men to leave the cave and surrender.[7] This latest group brought the total Attu prisoner count to twenty-six.

How many surviving Japanese wandered and died among the mountains was never known. However, in mid-July, four starving Japanese were sighted[8] but they disappeared before they could be overtaken. In late August, one of them was captured.[9] Two weeks later, another was taken, and a third soon after.[10] The fourth man vanished and was not seen again.

**ALTHOUGH THE APRIL 1942 DOOLITTLE RAID** on Japan had been a shock to the Japanese people, Tokyo downplayed any setbacks that the Japanese forces encountered during the first year of the war. Now, with the announcement of the loss of Attu, Tokyo was revealing that the war, especially in the North Pacific, was not going as well as expected.[11]

Radio Tokyo began to put a patriotic face on the defeat. Domestic broadcasts repeatedly made special mention of Colonel Yamasaki, whose leadership inspired the defense of Attu and turned the members of the annihilated garrison into national heroes. The broadcasts announced the emperor's recognition of the men's sacrificial devotion to the nation. Yamasaki was posthumously promoted two ranks, from colonel to lieutenant general.[12] Yamasaki and twenty-five of his officers and men also were cited for "conspicuous gallantry A." Commander Emoto of the naval unit on Attu and sixteen of his officers and men received the same citation.[13]

In 1944, on the first anniversary of the Japanese sacrifice on Attu, the emperor awarded additional citations and decorations to "heroes of the army, navy, merchant marine, and civilian employees of the Attu garrison." Maj. Tokuo Kobayashi and 135 men of the shipping unit were posthumously decorated with the Order of the Golden Kite. Twenty-seven civilians were given the same award. In Yamanashi Prefecture, the birthplace of Colonel Yamasaki, an estimated 100,000 Japanese attended a memorial service for their fallen hero.[14]

★ ★ ★

**IMMEDIATELY AFTER THE ATTU BATTLEFIELD** was silenced, nisei began translating various documents found on the torn Japanese bodies. Only personal documents were discovered because Yamasaki had ordered that all official papers be destroyed before his men embarked on the banzai charge.

Figure 4. "Somewhere in the Aleutians" (Adak, 1943)—Chikara Don Oka and
Mitsuru Shibata.

Other nisei began to interrogate the Japanese prisoners in greater
depth. And still other nisei were given roles to play before and during the planned invasion of Kiska scheduled for August 15.

During the battle, Chikara Don Oka was on Adak, where he was
attached to the G-2 Japanese map section (Figure 4). From current
intelligence he transferred data to maps so rapidly and effectively
that he was awarded a special commendation. After the battle, he
was attached to the Alaska Scouts for the coming Kiska operation.
According to plan, Oka was prepared, again using current intelligence, to make quick map sketches pinpointing the exact enemy
concentrations to be neutralized. When Kiska was found to be

evacuated, the Scouts searched the island for discarded Japanese documents for Oka to translate and determine their intelligence value.[15]

A joint American-Canadian amphibious task force (JTF-9) was assembled for the Kiska operation. Nobuo Furuiye reported for duty with the Canadian Grenadiers, who lacked a Japanese linguist.[16]

In the lull after the Attu battle, Frank Imon served as an interpreter at the Japanese prisoner of war compound. He recalled:

> [T]here was a very officious Japanese noncommissioned officer who made life unpleasant for his fellow prisoners. They planned retaliation. We had obtained a fifty-gallon metal drum for their bathing purposes. The drum was filled with water each day. The water was heated by a coal-burning fire under the drum. The non-com, being the senior-ranking prisoner, always used his authority to be the first to enjoy it. To protect each bather from the hot bottom of the heated drum, a wooden pallet was put on the drum's floor. One day, the POWs carefully removed the pallet from the drum and then watched their sergeant step on the hot metal. During the ensuing commotion, the guards called for me, and it was some show! This non-com, stark naked and with a flowing beard, chased every POW in sight!

As the Kiska August 15 D-Day approached, Imon and other nisei were placed aboard a prison ship to await the arrival of the additional Japanese prisoners expected from the Kiska conquest.[17]

Captain White assigned other I&I nisei, including Ted Ishida, Shigeo Ito, Tedashi Ogawa, and Yoshio Morita, to accompany combat units during the expected battle. In the absence of any enemy troops on Kiska, the I&I men subsequently located unofficial "battle" booty in a cave filled with canned meat, seafood, fruit, and various other Japanese delicacies. The nisei avoided an order to seal the cave. Instead, they became their own chefs. The intelligence unit dined well for days.[18]

Having regained Attu and Kiska, the Aleutian campaign was completed. Until plans were made for further operations in the North Pacific, many of the Army and Navy units were being deployed from the Aleutians to other Pacific areas (see Chapter 6). Twenty of the battle-tested nisei were ordered from Alaska for reassignment. Other nisei would soon follow.[19] A small cadre was retained in Alaska for contingency use. Among those temporarily assigned to the cadre were Pete Nakao, Yashio Norita, Roy Ashizawa, and Hiroma William Wada (Figure 5).[20]

Some of the Aleutian nisei veterans were assigned to the Japanese Language Military Intelligence Service School and the Pentagon. However, most of them distinguished themselves in far-flung battle areas. Sent first to the Honolulu Annex to the Joint Intelligence Center Pacific Ocean Area (JICPOA) in Hawaii,[21] they were organized

Figure 6. Among the Aleutian campaign veterans who were returned to Fort Snelling for reassignment were *front row* (left to right): Mickey Kuroiwa, Juetts Kariya, and Nobuo Furuiye; *back row:* Chikara Don Oka, Yoshio Hotta, Roy Miyata. Photo courtesy Chikara Don Oka.

into new MIS teams for further service. Among the team leaders were Alaska veterans Nobuo Furuiye, Chikara Don Oka, and Tadashi Ogawa (Figure 6). Fellow veteran Roy Miyata was a member of one team. Other MIS teams accompanied U.S. Marine Corps units in various island conquests, including Saipan, Tinian, and Iwo Jima. George Hayashida joined General MacArthur's forces in New Guinea and later the Sixth Army intelligence staff.[22]

Shigeo Ito's ten-man nisei team, attached to the Army's Seventy-seventh Infantry Division, contained his fellow Alaska veterans Tetsuji Yamada and Mitsuru Shibata. The Seventy-seventh Division fought on Guam and then Leyte and Okinawa. During the latter campaign, Shibata was on the neighboring island of Ie Shima, where Ernie Pyle, the war correspondent, was killed. Shibata was trying to guide a group of island refugees to safety when a sniper killed him, too. Shibata was the only nisei from the Aleutians to die in action during the war. Two other Aleutian campaign veterans, Howard Nakamura and Juetts Kariya, were assigned to serve beyond the Pacific in the China-Burma-India theater of war.[23]

After the end of the Aleutian campaign, the name of one of the nisei, Yasuo Sam Umetani, would be especially long remembered. It was he who first translated the diary of Paul Nobuo Tatsuguchi, a doctor educated and licensed in American whose body and diary were found on Attu. Umetani wept when he read the diary's final passage containing Tatsuguchi's poignant farewell message to his wife and two daughters. Umetani never realized that the diary's translation would launch a controversy that has never been entirely resolved (see Chapter 5).

# Chapter Five

# The Tatsuguchi Diary

T HE DIARY OF DR. PAUL NOBUO TATSUGUCHI, found in the Attu battlefield litter, proved to be the only surviving Japanese record of the desperate battle that ended in a final banzai charge. Although it was futile, the banzai charge nonetheless became an example for other inspired Japanese island defenders to follow later in the Pacific war.[1]

During the concluding fury of the Attu battle on May 30, Tatsuguchi emerged from the cave where his field hospital was located. Two American soldiers saw him. "Don't shoot!" Tatsuguchi shouted in English. He waved a Bible. "Don't shoot! I am a Christian!" One soldier heard the shout over the battle noise and the whistling Attu wind. The other soldier did not. He apparently mistook the Bible for a weapon, and killed the unarmed doctor.[2]

Later, a document was found in Tatsuguchi's medical bag.[3] Since the document was handwritten in Japanese and therefore of possible intelligence value, it was sent directly to the I&I command post for examination. Here nisei Sergeant Umetani soon realized that the document contained Tatsuguchi's diary entries made during the three-week battle. As the battle neared its climax, Tatsuguchi made his final entry to confirm his Christian faith and to anticipate his own death.

Because it was a unique Japanese daily record of the battle, the diary was of immediate military interest. However, it later became the object of public speculation. The North Pacific security curtain that had curbed the flow of military information from the Alaskan combat zone suddenly leaked. Mail and media content, electronic communications, and public travel were all subject to controls. The hole that now developed in the security curtain was created by civilian crews of supply ships when they departed the Aleutian area. Crewmen smuggled copies of the diary translation, in demand as souvenirs, to the West Coast. Various versions of the translation began to appear in major American publications.

A portion of the translation led some readers to question how Tatsuguchi's wounded Japanese patients met their deaths. How did the hospitalized men die? Did Tatsuguchi in fact kill them?

Tatsuguchi became an enigma. To be sure, he was an American-educated and -licensed physician, but who was he really? The answers to these questions required a study of the influence of his missionary parents and his zeal to practice medicine as a medical missionary.

The Seventh-Day Adventist (SDA) church, heeding a strong commitment to education in California, established Heraldsburg College in 1882. The institution was later renamed Pacific Union College and relocated near Angwin. Its liberal arts curriculum was and still is designed "to prepare students for productive lives of useful service and uncompromising personal integrity."

The Tatsuguchi family home was in Hiroshima, Japan. Suichi Tatsuguchi came alone to San Francisco in 1895 "to explore the New World." He attended Heraldsburg College, where the SDA church baptized him, and then the College of Physicians and Surgeons in San Francisco, where he specialized in dentistry. Because he was convinced that medical missionary work in Japan was his destiny, he returned to Hiroshima in 1907 to fulfill it.

At home, Suichi married Sadako Shibata and soon had a popular and prosperous dental practice. He promoted the establishment of the Hiroshima SDA church, where his wife was the organist. In

1928, he used his popularity and wealth to support the founding of the SDA's Tokyo Sanitarium.

The Tatsuguchis had three sons and three daughters. Influenced by his parents, the eldest son, Kazuo, went to California to study at Pacific Union College. From California, he went to Europe, where he attended music conservatories in Paris and Berlin before returning to Japan.[4]

The middle son was Paul (although he was known as "Joseph" at home). Paul's family ties with the SDA church and the California SDA educational system made it inevitable that Paul should go to America and pursue his dream of becoming a medical missionary. He entered Pacific Union College in 1929 and was graduated in 1932. When his parents died unexpectedly, Paul returned to Japan to assist in settling the family affairs. Back in California in 1933, Paul commenced his medical studies at the College of Medical Evangelists at Loma Linda University. His classroom courses completed in 1937, he then accepted a year's internship at White Memorial Hospital in Los Angeles.

In the summer of 1938, he was awarded his doctor of medicine degree and California medical license. A position with the SDA Tokyo Sanitarium awaited him. Because he would be taking care of tuberculosis patients in Japan, he decided to spend additional months of postgraduate study in California. When he was finally ready to depart in 1939, he did so with his bride, Taeko Miyake,[5] the daughter of the SDA pastor in Honolulu (Figure 7).

In Tokyo, Paul and Taeko were keenly aware of the rising tensions between Japan and the United States. Paul tried to ignore the situation by concentrating on his Tokyo Sanitarium medical practice and, with Taeko, on the SDA church activities. In 1940, their daughter Misako was born. The international situation continued to deteriorate and pulled Paul's loyalties in opposite directions. He loved his native land but he could not ignore his feelings for America, to which he hoped someday to return.

Figure 7. Newlyweds Dr. Paul
Nobuo Tatsuguchi and his bride,
Taeko Miyake Tatsuguchi, 1938.
Photo courtesy Laura Tatsuguchi-
Davis.

Finally, in early 1941, the Japanese army ordered him to cease his medical practice and report for induction into the First Imperial Guard Regiment in Tokyo (Figure 8). In uniform as a private, he was garrisoned nearby so that he was able to visit Taeko and Misako on occasion.

Meanwhile, he was promoted to private first class and then to corporal. In September 1941, he entered the Japanese army medical school. Upon graduation, he was promoted to sergeant major, but the Japanese military medical authorities apparently remained suspicious of his American schooling and residence. Although they later granted him the courtesy title of acting medical officer, they never gave him official medical officer status.

Figure 8. Inducted into the Japanese army in 1941, Dr. Tatsuguchi was first assigned to the First Imperial Guard Regiment in Tokyo. Photo courtesy Laura Tatsuguchi-Davis.

When the Japanese armed forces reoccupied Attu in October 1942, Paul bade farewell to Taeko, now pregnant with their second child, and Misako. He could not reveal his destination to his family. However, Taeko recalled that Paul had been studying maps of the North Pacific area. At one point, he remarked that perhaps he might yet meet some of his school classmates![6]

Several weeks of silence followed. Finally, Taeko received a post-card. At the time of writing it, Paul was on an unnamed island (probably Paramushiro). Shortly afterward, Paul's military authorities delivered to Taeko a lock of Paul's hair. By Japanese custom, the hair prepared relatives in advance for a death when it would be impossible for a soldier's ashes to be returned to Japan. Therefore,

Taeko knew that Paul was being sent to a combat zone of high risk. She suspected that he was bound for either Attu or Kiska.

After Paul arrived on Attu, ships carrying supplies and mail were few and unscheduled because of American naval and air patrols. His outgoing mail—four letters and several postcards—was heavily censored. He was not allowed to disclose his location. He could not even indicate the date of his correspondence. Heeding these harsh restrictions, he reflected his love of nature by writing about such subjects as the changeable weather, the beauty of the snowy and mountainous landscape, and his success in finding and catching fish.

He was cheered when Taeko informed him that their second daughter, Mutsuko, had been born in February. Taeko also managed to send small packages containing cookies and medical creams. The latter were for Paul's personal use on his skin, chafed by Attu's winds.

On May 11, 1943, the American Seventh Infantry Division began landing troops on Attu, where Colonel Yamasaki's defending force waited in the fog and snow on the island's mountainsides. Paul moved his field hospital into a cave while treating the early battle casualties. During the lengthy battle that followed, he was forced to move his hospital from cave to cave as the American encirclement tightened.

Paul found time to maintain a diary of his observations from the moment the first American shot was fired. His diary entries until May 29 seemed unemotional in tone as he described the Japanese defensive tactics, the reaction of Japanese soldiers to the battle as the casualties mounted, and his own suffering. Only on May 29, when he made his farewell diary entry, did he mention his Christian beliefs and his love for his family as he faced the prospect of his own death.[7]

Because the Tatsuguchi diary was the sole Japanese daily eyewitness record of the defense of Attu, two diary entries especially caught the attention of American military authorities and the media: the entries on May 14 and May 29.

On May 12 and 13, American troops continued to land on Attu's shores. On May 14, Seventh Division artillery sought targets among the Japanese mountainside emplacements. Phosphorus smoke shells were fired and exploded to mark possible enemy positions. The smoke caused both Japanese and Americans to fear that their respective opponents were introducing poison gas.

In his May 14 diary entry, Paul, undoubtedly reflecting Japanese rumors, noted that the Americans were using gas, which was causing no harm since strong winds quickly dispersed it. On the same day, Sherman Montrose, a war correspondent for NEA-Acme Newspictures, accompanied a group of nervous American troops who had come ashore to engage the enemy for the first time. When a smoke shell exploded, the troops assumed that they were coming under a Japanese gas attack. They then panicked and prepared to return to their landing craft. Montrose rallied the troops. After he convinced them that the smoke was not poison gas, they resumed the attack.[8]

On May 29, after the deadly struggle had raged day after day, Colonel Yamasaki prepared his surviving men for one last desperate effort to break through the American encirclement. Although most of his May 29 diary entry was his farewell message to his family, Paul wrote, according to one translation, that "all the patients in the hospital were made to commit suicide." Another translation contained a statement that implied that he had taken care of all patients with grenades. (A copy of one of the early translations is in Appendix C.)

General Buckner was concerned that the diary's May 14 entry might mistakenly indicate that American forces had used poison gas on Attu. Although he had seen only one translation, he ordered that Tatsuguchi's Japanese-language diary be sent to his headquarters and that all copies of the translation be confiscated. His order was too late. Various "souvenir" translations had already been circulating in the Aleutians even while the seizure of Kiska was being planned.

The original Tatsuguchi diary never reached Buckner's headquarters. It simply vanished. The frustrated Alaska Defense Command G-2 finally reported in early September that "incidents of
unauthorized possession of captured Japanese documents from
Attu have been noted recently in Alaska and the United States
which has resulted in tightening security measures in Alaska. A
Navy translation of a captured Japanese diary has been reported to
have reached the Alaska mainland and the United States where
copies have been offered by merchant seamen for sale to publishing
agencies."[9]

At least ten different versions of the translated diary were
discovered in the United States. Although some sentences were
identical in a few versions, whole sentences were omitted in others.
Garbled Japanese words were often used in lieu of English equiva-
lents. Ordinary English-language typographical errors were common. The original diary itself had been handwritten in Japanese
characters, probably in haste during times of stress. Family members
later reported that Paul's Japanese handwriting under the best of
conditions was not skillful. Any slight changes in the composition
of written characters could have led the translators to altogether different meanings.

American newspapers and magazines promptly exploited the sen-
sational aspects of the diary's content. Although noting the historical significance of the document, editors placed emphasis on the fact
that an American-educated and -licensed doctor was with the
Japanese army on Attu. They especially noted that the doctor who
professed a belief in Christ may have killed the wounded patients
on the eve of the final banzai charge.

Only a skillful retranslation of his diary would serve to clarify
what Tatsuguchi actually wrote during the last frantic days of the
battle. A half century later, speculation still remained that his original diary might exist in an overlooked container in some military or
university archive. From the time when the various translations first
became public in 1943, however, the people who knew Tatsuguchi

best staunchly defended his memory. His family, his college and medical school classmates, and the wide community of Seventh-Day Adventists all pointed out that he was a dedicated pacifist who had carefully prepared himself to serve his church as a medical missionary. They were certain that the gentle doctor they knew and loved found himself on Attu in a situation beyond his control. They believed that his true actions, whatever they were, did not violate his religious and medical creeds.[10]

It was a cruel twist of fate that, although Tatsuguchi foresaw the probability that he would die on Attu, his Bible may have been mistaken for a weapon and thus caused his death.

# THE KURILE ISLANDS

★　★　★

# 1943–1945

# Chapter Six

# Looking Beyond the Aleutians

**W**HILE THE ALEUTIAN CAMPAIGN was nearing its finish, General Buckner was expressing his wish to "walk through the ashes of Tokyo." To his superiors, he argued that the Aleutians should be the route for a northern invasion through the Kurile Islands to Hokkaido. Realistically, he knew that the use of such an invasion route would require the establishment of a forward base on Kamchatka. Although the Soviet Union was still adhering to its 1941 neutrality pact with Japan, Buckner nonetheless set staff officers to work on strategic studies of the Kamchatka–Kurile Islands area.

Military intelligence officers in the Aleutians had scant information regarding the extent and size of the Japanese installations in the northern Kuriles. Washington officials approved an Eleventh Air Force proposal to make two aerial probes of the area in July 1943. The exploratory raids, however, managed to alert the Japanese to the danger of American long-range bombers capable of flying 750 miles to the Kuriles and returning to their Aleutian bases. The startled Japanese called for fighter support and prepared to counter the next American foray.[1]

In the military sense, Paramushiro and Shumushu islands were now essential parts of the Japanese northern homeland. Together, they comprised the topmost fortress of the Japanese defenses and the main barricade against U.S. invasion from Alaska or even

Kamchatka. About 5,200 Japanese military and civilian personnel, having been evacuated from Kiska without American knowledge, arrived safely in the northern Kuriles on August 1. Japanese army men reinforced the garrison at the Kashiwabara staging area on Para-mushiro, and the navy personnel moved into the Kataoka naval base on neighboring Shumushu. They were promptly added to the work-force engaged in constructing hasty defense fortifications and air-craft landing strips.[2]

On August 12 (Kurile time), nine Eleventh Air Force bombers again approached the Kurile combat area.[3] They encountered a swarm of fighters that destroyed one bomber and damaged another so badly that it was unable to return to its Aleutian base. Seeking a landing site on nearby Kamchatka, the bomber crash-landed not far from Petropavlovsk with only one fatality. The Soviet Border Patrol (NKVD) interned the surviving ten crew members.[4]

In the wake of the Japanese abandonment of Kiska, Adm. Chester Nimitz (CINCPAC), seeing no immediate threat of a Japanese coun-terattack, dissolved the joint Army-Navy Aleutian campaign task force headed by Vice Adm. Thomas C. Kinkaid. He returned the Navy's North Pacific Force under Vice Adm. Frank Jack Fletcher to a traditional Navy role. Kinkaid himself departed to take command of the Seventh Fleet in support of General MacArthur's offensive in the South Pacific. General Buckner retained his military authority in Alaska.[5]

Many of the Army air force and ground units that had been assembled for the Kiska assault began to move from the Aleutians to other theaters of war. With them went most of the accredited war correspondents.[6]

On October 5, the Joint Chiefs of Staff (JCS), after studying the current situation in the war with Japan, decided that, contrary to the northern route offensive that Buckner advocated, the number of Buckner's personnel would be reduced from the current 120,000 to 80,000 by July 1, 1944, with the possibility of further reductions at a later time. In the view of the JCS, an invasion of the Kurile Islands seemed unlikely unless or until the Soviet Union entered the war against Japan.

However, assuming that an invasion of the Kuriles should become feasible or necessary, the JCS set a target date of spring 1945 for the proposed campaign. To support that contingency, the JCS authorized the construction of Aleutian staging areas and warehousing for a task force of 50,000 men on Adak and improved air base facilities for possible B-29 operations on Adak, Amchitka, and Shemya. Defense contractors with their heavy equipment and civilian workmen soon began arriving to undertake the massive projects.[7]

Buckner's immediate concern was to insure that the security curtain concealing the new activity in the Aleutians remained intact. The military restrictions in Alaska during the 1942–1943 Aleutian campaign had been so strict that in the continental United States, public concern for and interest in the war in the North Pacific had been stifled. In Alaska, public concern remained high but resentment of the continued restrictions simmered. With the Japanese invaders no longer in the Aleutians, Buckner decided to relax a small portion of his restrictions. Military and civilian personnel under Army jurisdiction in Alaska, exclusive of the Aleutian area, could now reveal their precise geographic locations by place name. However, troops and civilians in the Aleutians could disclose their location only by the term "Somewhere in the Aleutian Area."[8]

Shortly after the JCS postponed consideration of a northern route invasion, the War Department announced the establishment of the Alaskan Department, effective November 1. Unlike the Alaska Defense Command that it replaced, the Alaskan Department was not an appendage of the Western Defense Command. Instead, it was an independent command directly responsible to the War Department. One of the Alaskan Department's first actions was to eliminate another of the unpopular civilian restrictions. The requirement for conducting "dim-outs in certain areas of the Territory of Alaska" was suspended but subject to resumption if deemed necessary.[9]

While preparing to defend the Kuriles, the Japanese were handicapped by not knowing at what point in time, whether it be in the immediate or distant future, an American invasion force might strike. Unlike the Japanese, however, the Americans entered a waiting period of at least eighteen months before initiating an invasion.

During this waiting period, American aerial bombardment and naval surface harassment, together with deception operations, would apply increasing pressure on the Kurile defenders. Army engineers and Navy SeaBees quickly completed new forward air bases on Attu and nearby Shemya Island. These bases became the launching points for the Eleventh Air Force and Fleet Air Wing Four bombing raids to the Kuriles for the remaining years of the war.

*Chapter Seven*

# American Prisoners in the Kuriles

**A** **PORTION OF THE AMERICAN MILITARY FORCE** was relocated following the end of the Aleutian campaign. The Eleventh Air Force lost four of its six bombardment squadrons. The remaining bombardment squadrons were the Seventy-seventh (B-25 medium bombers) and the 404th (B-24 heavy bombers). The B-25 bomber normally carried a crew of five and the B-24 bomber a crew of eleven, although observers were occasionally added. To the diminished Eleventh Air Force fell the Army's share of the responsibility for carrying the war to the Kuriles. The Navy's share was vested in the Fleet Air Wing Four, with its rotating VPB-131, VB-135, VB-136, and VB-139 fighter-bomber squadrons. The Navy's PV-1 and PV-2 bomb loads were comparable to those carried by the Army's B-25s. Each fighter-bomber carried a crew of five or six.[1]

The cost of bringing the war to the Kuriles was high. To complete the long flight to and from the Kuriles, the bombers endured frigid, turbulent weather that often turned deadly. Other bombers, due to mechanical problems or fuel exhaustion, simply disappeared. Although the Japanese were able to shoot down some of the American raiders, they often damaged others so severely that their crews were unable to return to their distant Aleutian bases. Instead, to avoid capture by the Japanese, the flyers crash-landed on the nearby Kamchatkan Peninsula, usually in the vicinity of Petropavlovsk.

The Soviet Union, as a declared neutral in the war with Japan, interned the American crews. During the ensuing two years (1943–1945), beginning with the ten Army airmen already interned following the earlier August 12 raid, an additional 232 airmen aboard thirty-one Army and Navy bombers from the Aleutians were interned at Petropavlovsk and then moved thousands of miles across Siberia to a holding camp near Tashkent, Uzbekistan. With NKVD help, the internees later "escaped" into Iran after being sworn to secrecy.[2]

The Japanese did not capture any of the Fleet Air Wing Four's airmen. However, a number of Eleventh Air Force survivors from totally disabled bombers, unable to reach Kamchatka, became the only American airmen to fall into Japanese hands during the war.

In the first three exploratory raids in July and August, the Eleventh Air Force had already encountered the hazards of reaching and attacking the northern Kuriles. On September 12 (Kurile time), a month after suffering its first losses, the Eleventh Air Force organized another strike, this one to be massive. All available bombers—twelve B-25s and seven B-24s—were mustered and launched.

The resulting battle was a major disaster that would stagger the Eleventh Air Force for months to come. When the raiders approached Paramushiro, the Japanese defenders were waiting for them. The 404th's B-24s were scheduled to drop their bombs from high altitudes. The Seventy-seventh's B-25s, led by squadron commander Maj. Richard Salter, descended to deck level in order to hurl their bombs against cargo and naval vessels. Flying abreast while skimming the ocean's surface, the B-25s presented fearsome but vulnerable targets for the Japanese defenders. In the month since the mid-August raid, the Japanese had reinforced their array of anti-aircraft guns and added even more fighters. Now, during the ensuing melee, the Japanese downed one B-24[3] and two B-25s. Two other B-24s and five B-25s were so badly crippled that they were forced to limp to Kamchatka and internment.[4]

The remaining nine battered bombers managed to deliver their exhausted and bloody crews to their Aleutian bases. The survivors reported seeing an out-of-control B-24 plunge into the sea. Lt. Albert W. Berecz was pilot of one of the lost B-25s.[5] His bomber was flying to the left of Major Salter's lead plane when Berecz's bomber was sprayed with gunfire. An engine burst into flames, and the bomber soon vanished.[6] The second B-25, piloted by Lt. Quinton D. Standiford,[7] was on the right of Salter's bomber. Hit by an anti-aircraft gun burst, Standiford's B-25 exploded into a ball of fire. Flaming debris splashed into the water. It seemed impossible that any person could have survived, and the Eleventh Air Force so assumed.

However, one member of the crew did escape from the flaming wreckage: the radioman and tail gunner Sgt. Francis Leonard McEowen (Figure 9). Two days after the raid, Radio Tokyo boasted of McEowen's capture.[8]

Two months later, on November 14, Radio Tokyo again addressed the subject of McEowen's capture, this time in a lengthy interview allegedly with McEowen himself. In the broadcast, the American revealed details of his rescue and appreciation for the fishermen who found him and saved his life. Eleventh Air Force intelligence officers nonetheless remained skeptical that McEowen could have lived through a midair explosion. They suspected that McEowen's name and serial number as quoted could have been obtained from McEowen's identification tags found on his corpse.[9]

The Radio Tokyo broadcast, however, triggered a fresh Eleventh Air Force investigation. The report, rendered on March 10, 1944, officially concluded that the broadcast was an elaborate hoax that the Japanese concocted from documents found on McEowen's body. The investigators were confident that only a miracle would have allowed any man to escape death in the fiery crash. They recommended that Sergeant McEowen's status be changed from missing in action to killed in action.[10]

Nonetheless, Sergeant McEowen was very much alive. Although not acknowledged by historians, he was Japan's first American

Figure 9. S. Sgt. Francis Leonard McEowen prior to his disastrous mission to the Kuriles in September 1943. He was the first Eleventh Air Force airman to be captured by the Japanese. Photo courtesy Mary Louise McEowen.

prisoner of war from the Eleventh Air Force. That McEowen survived the bomber's destruction indeed seemed a miracle. During the raid, he was in the "bubble" at the bomber's tail. When the plane exploded, it broke apart. He was trapped inside the tail section, which plunged into the sea and immediately sank. Instinctively freeing himself from the sinking wreckage, he struggled to reach the surface. The frantic effort seemed endless. A fishing boat was nearby, and the Japanese fishermen saw McEowen's head when it suddenly appeared.

They rescued him and took him to the shore. He was in a state of shock due to exposure to the frigid water, and he had a deep gash below one knee caused by the jagged edge of the tail wreckage.[11]

To bolster civilian morale, Japanese domestic media, both radio and newspaper, exploited McEowen's capture with photographs and embellished interviews.[12] During his lengthy solitary confinement on Paramushiro, his leg injury went untreated and he endured continued interrogation. Later, after passing through a series of POW camps in Japan, McEowen was moved to Tokyo, where he labored in the Sumidagawa railroad yards.

The Eleventh Air Force, at first stunned by the loss of nearly half of its available bombers, began a program of replacement and retraining of both aircraft and crews. While licking its wounds, however, it looked forward to the time when it would again undertake the long missions to harass the Kuriles.

Meanwhile, the Fleet Air Wing Four tested and confirmed the long-range capability of its fighter-bombers to join the Kurile fray. At the same time, when weather conditions permitted, both Army and Navy aircraft conducted regular searches of the North Pacific area between the Aleutians and the Kuriles.

During the summer, autumn, and winter of 1944, the number of Army and Navy missions to the Kuriles continued to increase. Although there was also a rising number of crash landings on Kamchatka with the resulting inevitable internments, the only Americans to fall into the hands of the Japanese in 1944 were members of another Army B-25 bomber crew.

On September 10 (Kurile time), two B-25 bombers, piloted by Lt. William Head[13] and Lt. Albert Scott,[14] were on a mission to seek and destroy Kurile coastal shipping. Skimming the ocean's surface, Scott's bomber approached its target freighter too low and clipped the vessel's mast. Lt. Ralph Hammond, Head's copilot, recalled watching Scott's B-25 "mushing into the mast, the bomber's tail getting knocked off, and the wrecked plane then splashing into the water. We saw members of Scott's crew getting into a life raft."[15]

After repatriation at war's end, Scott reported that a Japanese trawler rescued three crew members and carried them to Paramushiro. They were then transferred to POW camps in Japan.[16] Of the original crew of six, the three men who lived through the crash and subsequent prison confinement were Lt. Albert Scott, F.O. William Gallo, and Sgt. Reynald Isrussi.[17] Following Scott's B-25 crash, Head's B-25 was then damaged when an anti-aircraft shell struck and destroyed one of its engines, forcing the pilot and his crew to find haven in Kamchatka.

In the closing months of the war in May–July 1945, two other Army bombers furnished Japan with the last American prisoners of war from the North Pacific. On May 20 (Kurile time), Lt. Raymond Lewis's B-25 was engaged in a raid on enemy installations and a fish cannery on Shumushu. His crew included his copilot, F.O. Edward Burrows; Lt. Milton Zack, navigator-bombardier; Cpl. William Bradley, radio gunner; Sgt. Robert Trant, engineer gunner; and Cpl. Walter Bailey, Sr., tail gunner. "We were still over water and could see Shumushu's coast when the Japanese fighters attacked," Zack later recalled. "Our plane shuddered and shook, and it felt as if we had hit a brick wall. . . . I looked to the right and could not believe my eyes. There was no propellor on the right engine. . . . I salvoed the bombs because I knew we were crashing on Shumushu. We bellied through two feet of snow. All six of us got out with no broken bones or serious injuries."[18]

A B-24 on a photographic mission over Shumushu located the skid marks leading to the crashed bomber. Another photographic mission a week later revealed that the bomber had been dismantled.[19]

The bomber crashed about two miles from the Kataoka naval base. The crew, expecting the Japanese to arrive soon, had time to destroy documents and personal papers. The six men had no choice but to surrender after the Japanese soldiers struggled through deep snow to reach them. The captives were taken to an underground barracks, where they spent the night on the freezing floor without blankets or food.[20]

The next morning they were marched to the naval base docks. They were handcuffed, blindfolded, and put aboard a ship that carried them to the nearby Paramushiro army staging area. They were locked in separate cells. Food was scant and the cells' facilities were primitive. After a week, about May 28, Lewis, Burrows, and Bradley vanished from their cells. Zack later learned from the Japanese that the three men had been placed on a ship bound for Hokkaido. While en route, the ship was sunk by an American submarine. There were no survivors.

About three days after Lewis, Burrows, and Bradley disappeared, Zack himself was handcuffed, blindfolded, and put aboard a Japanese plane. When it landed, Zack did not know where he was. He later learned that he was in Sapporo, Hokkaido.

Zack lost track of the time, but sometime in early June both Trant and Bailey arrived safely aboard a ship from Paramushiro. The three of them were lodged in separate cells. Disease and lack of food took their toll, but all three were still alive when Japan surrendered.[21]

On June 16 (Kurile time), two B-24 bombers were on attack missions west of Paramushiro. Lt. Richard Brevik was pilot of one and Lt. Carl Kulva, the other. Three enemy ships were sighted.[22] On Brevik's order, Cpl. William Cavanaugh, who was the bomber's armorer, pulled the pins to activate the bombs' instantaneous fuses. The bombardier salvoed all six 500-pound bombs. The immediate result was a tremendous explosion that shattered the aircraft.[23]

Kulva, in the second B-24, realized that Brevik's bomber had crashed in the ocean. When the cloud of spray settled, he saw that the bomber was upside down, broken and sinking. Kulva completed his bomb run against the target ships and then returned to the crash site. He could not find any trace of wreckage or life rafts.[24]

After the explosion under Brevik's plane, Cavanaugh had time to reach the flight deck before the bomber hit the water. He, together with Brevik and the copilot, was thrown into the sea through the windshield, which had peeled open "like a can of sardines." When Cavanaugh came to the surface, Brevik also bobbed up a short distance away. Cavanaugh found an inflated life raft for himself and also managed to pull Brevik into it. Brevik was conscious but in severe pain due to internal injuries. There were no other survivors.

Brevik died the next morning. During the evening of the following day, June 18, Cavanaugh heard a noise. Alerted, he then saw a Japanese destroyer a half mile away. He fired a signal flare to attract attention. The warship approached and took him aboard. He was blindfolded and delivered to the Kataoka naval base on Shumushu. After three days of questioning, Cavanaugh was shipped to Japan.[25]

The fierce Japanese defense of the Kuriles was expected to cause the loss of some American aircraft with their crews. However, the unpredictable weather, more than any other factor, caused by far the greatest loss of American lives and created hardship and misery in carrying the war to the enemy in the North Pacific.

*Chapter Eight*

# Whither the North Pacific Weather?

**K**NOWN WEATHER STANDARDS and statistics were of little benefit in the North Pacific. On any given day, the weather varied in ways that were often unbelievable.[1] The summer air, however, was mild when compared to the violent conditions in winter.

The major weather problems in summer were fog and the force and direction of winds. Most of the storm centers in summer moved northeast from Japan toward the Bering Sea off Kamchatka. The area south of Kamchatka, including the Kurile Islands, had the reputation of being the foggiest area of the entire northern hemisphere in summer.

Spring and autumn were seasons of weather transition, and both had many satisfactory days for flying. However, the autumn conditions were somewhat better than those in spring. In winter, fog was less frequent, but successful flying was hampered by other weather hazards. Temperatures aloft were low and wind velocities were often high, especially in the upper altitudes. The result was turbulence, icing, and errors, sometimes fatal, in navigation and altitude settings.[2]

Unexpected squalls known as "williwaws" also provided special hazards to sea and air navigation. Columns of spray and mist resulting from williwaws frequently resembled swirling waterfalls. Williwaws could quickly change in direction and velocity, with gusts reaching over 100 miles per hour. The Aleutian weather therefore became a foremost problem for American as well as Japanese military operations. However, the Japanese enjoyed one advantage. Because weather usually moved from west to east, the Japanese knew in advance what general weather conditions would likely prevail in the Aleutians.[3]

BEFORE WORLD WAR II COMMENCED, the principal problem with weather forecasting in the North Pacific was the delay in transmitting weather data, meager at best, from three nearby weather stations—Atka in the Aleutians, St. Paul in the Pribilof Islands, and Bethel in southwestern Alaska.[4] As the Army and Navy began to react to the developing crisis between Japan and the United States, the Army Air Corps activated a weather detachment at Ladd Field near Fairbanks in January 1941. In May, its headquarters was moved to Elmendorf Field near Anchorage. The Navy followed with the establishment of its Fleet Weather Central at Kodiak in October 1941.[5] After the Pearl Harbor attack, the Army weather detachment was redesignated as the Eleventh Air Corps Squadron, Weather, and then as the Eleventh Weather Squadron in support of the Eleventh Air Force. The squadron reached its peak expansion in 1943, with fifty weather stations, most of which were in or adjacent to the Aleutians.[6]

Both the Army and Navy rushed to develop weather service networks in the future North Pacific battle zone. The U.S. Weather Service and the Civil Aviation Administration loaned equipment and personnel to support the early military weather service expansion efforts.

The original Army plan called for weather service stations throughout the Alaska mainland as well as in the Aleutians. However, when war erupted, the military situation caused an abrupt shift in the plan. The priorities for weather stations in the central, eastern, and northern parts of the mainland were immediately downgraded. Instead, available supplies, equipment, and personnel were diverted to the Aleutians, the Alaska Peninsula, and the southeastern portion of Alaska.[7]

Two military weather stations in the Aleutians became operational in late May 1942, a week before the Japanese struck at Dutch Harbor. One was the Navy's on Kiska, and the other was the Army's on Umnak Island near Dutch Harbor. Although the Japanese occupation silenced the station on Kiska, the Umnak Island station's weather services helped American pilots to surprise the Dutch Harbor raiders.[8]

With the Japanese seizure of the weather station on Kiska, little information was available concerning the weather in the enemy-held area that was four flying hours west of Umnak. The only data came from aircraft sent especially on weather reconnaissance prior to bomber mission departures, or from surface vessels ranging westward. Under these circumstances, trustworthy predictions were practically impossible. Serious Army and Navy aircraft operational losses were the result.[9]

The situation remained unchanged for three months until the American military landing and occupation of Adak on August 30. Both the Army and Navy established weather stations there in October. As a result, better weather information became available and forecasts more accurate. Weather reports could now be obtained over 300 miles deeper into the Aleutian area than when the Umnak station was the last one westward. Beyond Adak, however, the weather map lacked reliability until American forces occupied Amchitka and a weather station was installed there in January 1943.

In March 1943, the Army and Navy combined their weather operations on Adak and established a Joint Weather Central to serve both Army air and Navy air and surface craft. Weather analyses and forecasts for surface and upper air became available for current and future operations against the enemy on Kiska and Attu.[10]

By this time, the air base was completed on Amchitka, only sixty-five miles from Japanese-held Kiska. The bombing of Kiska and Attu intensified. To support these assaults, information for weather forecasts was collected in an orderly fashion throughout the North

Pacific. Area search sectors were designated and daily air patrols were made when weather permitted. Each patrol pilot was required to relay in-flight radio weather reports to Adak Weather Central, and postflight reports were made after landing. The Eleventh Air Force Bomber Command now routinely dispatched a weather plane prior to launching missions. Navy surface vessels also continued to pass weather reports to Adak. Radio intelligence intercept stations also supplied enemy reports of weather conditions. Therefore, with the help of Fleet Air Wing Four, whose patrol craft also covered the various search sectors, the Bomber Command's weather plane, the Navy's surface vessels, and the radio intelligence intercept reports, predictions of impending weather became increasingly acceptable.[11]

The Eleventh Weather Squadron activated its first Attu station on June 7, 1943, a week after enemy resistance was shattered. It was placed on Massacre Bay's Alexai Point. Sporadic fighting with a few isolated Japanese hiding in the mountains continued, especially near Holtz Bay and Chichagof Harbor. Guards were posted at the weather station primarily to protect food supplies from hungry enemy foragers. One Japanese soldier was killed a mile from the station.

The new station immediately set to work on a series of forecasts for the Eleventh Air Force's initial bombing missions to the northern Kuriles. They were used on the July 10, July 18, August 11, and September 11 raids on Paramushiro and Shumushu.

Meanwhile, in conjunction with the rapid air base construction on nearby Shemya, a weather station was activated there on June 21.

A second Attu weather station became operational at Holtz Bay on August 12. It exchanged data with the Alexai Point station by telephone. However, the facility was short-lived; it was removed from service on October 31 following the occupation of Kiska.

Despite the confusion and shipping congestion at Kiska during the island's mid-August occupation, essential equipment was unloaded and assembled so that the Kiska weather station became operational after September 6. Another station on Buldir Island between Kiska and Attu was activated on October 14.

A new Army air base at Attu's Casco Cove required additional weather service support and a station was activated on January 6, 1944. It soon became the Army's principal source of weather data and prediction on Attu. The pioneer Alexai Point station was reduced to satellite status.

The Navy also placed two weather stations on Attu, one at Cape Wrangell and the other at Casco Cove. The latter was adjacent to but separate from the Army station.[12]

Once rid of the Japanese presence in the Aleutians, both the Army and Navy concentrated on the long-range aerial and surface harassment of the Kuriles during 1943–1945. The Eleventh Air Force and Fleet Air Wing Four launched their bombers from Attu and Shemya. Weather predictions made from the Attu and Shemya Weather Centrals continued to be vital. Greatest possible forecasting accuracy was required because the bombers often flew through marginal weather in order to take advantage of every opportunity to worry the enemy.[13]

Essential weather information consisted of reliable forecasts for (1) conditions at the Aleutian home bases at the times of departure and expected return, (2) conditions en route during the 1,500-mile flights to the Kuriles and return, and (3) conditions over the Kurile target areas.

Using all available sources of weather information, forecasters made a credible score of predicting the varied conditions that aircraft crews later encountered. The best forecasting record was established during March 1944, with a score of 94 percent. The poorest record was made during August 1944, with a score of 60 percent. However, the weather for the Kurile missions was correctly predicted as flyable or not flyable 71 percent of the time.[14]

Since weather controlled the decision for launching bombing missions from Attu and Shemya, each Weather Central presented a general weather briefing to the senior staff officers early every morning. Then, if a decision was "go," a detailed weather briefing was given to the crews being readied for mission departures.

To analyze firsthand weather information and to reassure the flying crew members, each forecaster also became a flying weather
observer. He volunteered for a place on a flight roster to accompany
a scheduled bomber crew to the Kuriles. In addition, if any pilot
questioned the accuracy of the weather forecast in the preflight
briefing, the forecaster was duty-bound to fly with the pilot.[15]

Weather observers thus shared the danger inherent in making the
long-range bombing raids. Among the members of bomber crews
listed as missing in action, five were volunteer weather observers.

Lt. Lee T. Harder was the Eleventh Air Force Bomber Command
assistant staff weather officer (Figure 10). He was lost on March 27,
1944, somewhere between the Aleutians and the Kuriles. In the last
radio communication with his Shemya base, the pilot reported that
his B-24 bomber had encountered icing and turbulent weather.[16]

On March 29, 1944, Aerographers Mate Jack Partier, Jr., was a
Navy weather observer aboard a Fleet Air Wing Four PV-1 that also
was reported missing in action after a raid on Shumushu.[17]

A month later, a B-24 was sent toward the Kuriles on weather
reconnaissance. Accompanying the bomber's crew was Capt.
Edward P. McDermott, the Eleventh Air Force Bomber Command's
newly appointed staff weather officer. The weather plane failed to
return to its Shemya base on April 26. It vanished without a trace.[18]

On November 6, 1944, Japanese fighters near the northern Kuriles
intercepted and destroyed a B-25 bomber from Attu. T. Sgt. James K.
Hastings was a weather observer on the ill-fated aircraft. Witnesses
reported that the bomber's wreckage immediately sank in the ocean
without any possible survivors.[19]

On December 7, 1944, 1st Lt. A. R. ("Bob") Miller, a weather
observer from Shemya Weather Central, was also listed as missing
in action (Figure 11). Unlike the other weather observers who met
tragic deaths in the North Pacific, Miller was the only weatherman
to be interned in Siberia. Assigned to Shemya Weather Central in
early September 1944, Miller immediately was involved in mission
weather forecasting and joined the volunteer weather observer pro-

Figure 10. Lt. Lee Harder was the first Eleventh Air Force weather observer to be missing in action. He was lost on a flight to the Kuriles on March 27, 1944. Photo courtesy Hal T. Spoden.

Figure 11. 1st Lt. A. R. ("Bob") Miller, weatherman on Shemya, September 18, 1944. In December, while on a Kurile mission with an Eleventh Air Force bomber crew, he became the only weather observer to be interned in Siberia. Photo courtesy A. R. Miller.

gram. He made his first flight to the Kuriles on September 18. He had completed fourteen such flights by early December. On December 6, he began his fifteenth flight with 2nd Lt. Robert A. Weiss's B-24 crew of twelve men.[20]

As the bomber neared the southern tip of Kamchatka en route to the northern Kuriles, the plane lost one of its engines and developed a major fuel leak. The disabled aircraft managed to reach and land near Petropavlovsk, as twenty-two other crippled Army and Navy bombers had done in the past.[21] During the internment procedures that followed, Soviet officials became suspicious of Miller's status. The Weiss bomber had thirteen men on it, not the twelve that had been aboard previously interned B-24 bombers. The officials knew that the pilot was usually the ranking officer of the crew, yet First Lieutenant Miller was one grade senior to Weiss and the bomber's other junior officers. When the Soviet interrogators learned that Miller's name was on the crew list as an "observer," they ceaselessly questioned him. Miller concluded that they suspected that he was an intelligence officer and that any response to their questions would inevitably lead to more questions. He limited his answers to "name, rank, and serial number." Later, when the crew was moved across Siberia to the internment holding camp near Tashkent, the questioning was resumed with the same results. Then, the disgruntled Soviet camp commander insisted that the uncooperative Miller, being the senior officer, assume responsibility for the behavior of the Weiss crew.

In addition to Miller and the twelve-man crew, thirty other American airmen were in the camp. Soviet officials and American diplomats arranged another "escape" to Tehran, Iran, where the forty-three airmen were released to American military officials.[22]

**THE MAJORITY OF THE WEATHERMEN** were far removed from contact with the enemy in the North Pacific. Nonetheless, many of them endured hazardous and lonely situations. Establishing and operating isolated weather reporting stations were challenges that in some cases led to disaster and even death.

One such fatal situation in the Aleutians developed on Chuginadak Island, located among the Islands of the Four Mountains, west of Umnak. Chuginadak, like all of the Aleutians, was volcanic. The island was blessed with not one but two volcanoes. One was extinct. The other, Mount Cleveland, was dormant, but at times its crater was known to emit lazy plumes of smoke. A saddle of flat land separated the bases of the two volcanoes, and an Eleventh Weather Squadron reporting station was established on the saddle.

In February 1944, a power barge with supplies for the station was scheduled to arrive. As the barge approached the island, severe weather ensued. As a result, the vessel ran aground somewhere on the island's coast. By radio, the four-man crew at the weather station was ordered to locate the grounded barge. The men divided themselves into two teams. They planned for the teams to relieve one another while making the search in the midst of eighty-mile-per-hour winds and freezing rain.

On the first team, Sgt. Wilfred Scarem eventually became too exhausted to return to the station for warmth and rest. His companion, Cpl. Clarence Clement, returned to the station to seek help for Scarem. While Clement rested at the station, Sgt. William Black and Cpl. George Bailey entered the storm to find Scarem. When Black and Bailey failed to return, the rested Clement reentered the storm to search for the three missing men. He found Scarem dead, the victim of exposure. Unable to locate the other two men, Clement reported the situation by radio. Rescue parties later arrived to search for the two lost men, to no avail. Finally, all hope gone, the weather station was evacuated.

A fresh five-man crew was assigned to reactivate the weather station. In early June 1944, Sgt. William Bigger went hunting and by accident found the remains of the two men missing since February.

The men apparently had lain down in the shelter of a huge rock to rest. They too had died of exposure.

On June 10, Sgt. Fred Purchase also decided to go hunting, this time on the slopes of Mount Cleveland. Meanwhile, the smoke from Mount Cleveland's crater was growing darker and heavier. Rumbles were heard at the station. Sgt. Alexander Alcantara and Cpl. Billy Cotton, knowing that Purchase's hearing was impaired, went to warn him of the danger. They were too late. Mount Cleveland erupted, sending lava and mud flows down its slopes. Alcantara and Cotton followed Purchase's boot tracks to a point where a mud slide covered them. The two men gave up the search when a fresh flow threatened to cut off their retreat.

When a rescue team arrived, a fruitless three-day search was made. No trace of Purchase was found. Because of the possibility of further eruptions, the Chuginadak Island weather station equipment was dismantled and removed.[23]

**VARIOUS SIBERIAN WEATHER REPORTS** enhanced the North Pacific weather maps to some extent. However, despite American encouragement, the Soviets were slow in developing weather reporting assets in eastern Siberia.[24]

Prior to World War II, the United States did not have access to weather information from Soviet sources. During his initial visit to Moscow in September 1941, Averell Harriman noted the need for an American-Soviet exchange of weather data. An agreement resulted in using San Francisco and Khabarovsk as the international weather exchange points. Reports from fewer than twenty existing weather stations in the whole of Siberia were available to Khabarovsk. However, even this meager collection of Siberian weather information, as opposed to no information at all, was an early Soviet contribution to understanding the weather menace in the North Pacific.

The flow of Siberian weather information improved slightly when the Alaska-Siberia (ALSIB) Air Ferry Route became operational in the winter of 1942–1943. Initially, an arrangement provided for the exchange of weather information between Irkutsk and Fairbanks. Later, the Soviets drastically limited the exchange to cover the weather conditions only on the ALSIB's Bering Sea route between Uel'kal and Nome.

Later, following negotiations at the Tehran Summit Conference in late 1943, a satisfactory arrangement for a complete Soviet-American exchange of weather information was reached in March 1944. However, the Soviets still lacked sufficient weather stations and communications to collect and report reliable data in and from the Soviet Far East.

As the U.S. forces began to converge on Japan's homeland, accurate and current weather information continued to assume major importance not only in the North Pacific but elsewhere. At the February 1945 Yalta Summit Conference, the U.S. Air Force offered Lend-Lease equipment so that the Soviets could establish thirty-five weather stations in eastern Siberia. The equipment was delivered during the summer of 1945, but the new stations' effectiveness was yet to be felt when the Potsdam Summit Conference was convened in July. The Soviets agreed to the U.S. Navy's proposal that two weather station liaison groups be established in the Soviet Far East, one at Khabarovsk and the other at Petropavlovsk. The two installations would be responsible for analyzing eastern Siberia's weather reports and communicating the results to the American forces in the Pacific. Two weather detachments were promptly dispatched to the Siberian sites.[25]

**IN ADDITION TO INTERCEPTING** Japanese radio weather reports from the Kuriles, American signal intelligence analysts in the Aleutians monitored enemy operational radio traffic in order to predict enemy intentions. (Appendix D contains a detailed discussion of signal intelligence operations.) Knowing that the Japanese also intercepted and analyzed American radio traffic, Aleutian-based intelligence specialists in 1944–1945 once again turned the tables on the Japanese. To deceive the enemy, false radio traffic in the Aleutians was employed in a deception scheme to excite the Japanese analysts regarding American plans for the Kuriles (see Chapter 9).

*Chapter Nine*

# American Deception and Japanese Reaction

**T**HE SIGNAL INTELLIGENCE OFFICIALS at Adak's Alaska Intelligence Center (AIC), having analyzed intercepted enemy radio traffic between Paramushiro and Kiska, reported on July 9, 1943, that they believed that the Japanese high command had decided to evacuate Kiska (see Appendix D). Later, a week after the American-Canadian landing on vacant Kiska, the AIC noted that the Japanese had doubled and then tripled high-priority message traffic involving Paramushiro, Sapporo (Hokkaido), and locations among the lesser Kurile Islands. Of special significance was traffic interpreted to indicate heavy shipping movements toward Paramushiro. The air corps radio traffic between Paramushiro and Sapporo was four times its normal load. In their estimate of the situation, Alaskan G-2 officials assumed that the Japanese recognized the possibility or even the probability that the American task force at Kiska could now be used for a major invasion of the Kuriles.[1]

Even though they destroyed three of the Eleventh Air Force's bombers in the September 12 raid on the Kuriles, the Japanese did not seem to be aware of the full extent of the American losses. Apparently expecting more American pressure on them, the Japanese made one last gesture of defiance. On October 6, AIC's signal intelligence analysts alerted the American bases in the western Aleutians to expect a large-scale enemy air raid in the immediate future.[2] Eight days later, on October 14, eight Japanese bombers flying at very high altitudes from Paramushiro arrived over Attu at twilight. They dropped a salvo of bombs across Massacre Bay to Alexai Point and then hastily departed. Several near misses but no direct hits were reported.[3]

Until mid-1943, the Japanese people were accustomed to hearing versions of "good" news regarding the war's progress. However, after the loss of Attu and Kiska, the Japanese government began to advise people of the war in more realistic terms by warning them of the approaching American encirclement. Continuing to glorify the deaths of the Attu defenders, Tokyo radio assured its Japanese audience that their sacrifices would lead to ultimate victory.

The October 14 Japanese token raid on Attu became a major media event in Japan.[4] Tokyo's *Nippon Times* published a long story with large headlines reading, "Attu Island Is Blasted Under Shower Of Japanese Bombs" and "Navy 'Wild Eagles' Defy Thick Fog and Bitter Cold In Attack On October 14." According to the story, an unstated number of navy bombers flew from an undisclosed North Pacific base and released their bombs on Attu's enemy positions. One of the bomber crews also dropped a "spirit-appeasing wreath," entrusted to the crew by an army unit, for the souls of the brave men who died gloriously defending the island. "The planes," the story added, "returned safely without the loss of a single one."[5]

G-2's review of the situation in the North Pacific noted the fierce Japanese defense of Paramushiro and Shumushu on September 12 and the Japanese response over Attu on October 14 as indications of a renewed Japanese combative mood. However, based on current intelligence analyses in November, the Japanese were not believed to be planning any further action against the Aleutians, nor were they believed any longer to be anticipating an immediate American assault on the Kuriles.[6] Nonetheless, American operations, plans, and preparations in the Aleutians continued to be objects of Japanese speculation. Tokyo radio repeatedly warned the people of American readiness to invade Japan from the north.

With the successful end of the Aleutian campaign and the disestablishment of the Alaska Defense Command, Alaskan newspaper editors were not content with continued military controls. While noting some modifications in the restrictions, they renewed their determined effort to have the security curtain, especially travel control, declared unnecessary. Nonetheless, being fully aware of the rising Japanese speculation regarding American intentions, General Buckner was determined to keep the security curtain intact.

Finally, the restless opponents of Alaska's military restrictions were cheered in early June 1944, when General Buckner officially departed Alaska. After four years of building and maintaining the security of the key North Pacific corner, the three-star general was being readied for greater leadership in the war with Japan.[7] In Alaska, Lt. Gen. Delos C. Emmons succeeded him.

Buckner's critics correctly anticipated that some changes were coming in Alaska. On August 1, the Alaskan Department announced a modification in the Alaska travel control policy[8]—one that, however, would not jeopardize the security curtain in the Aleutians.

Two new military control zones were established: Zone A embraced the Alaska mainland, Kodiak, and all of southeast Alaska. Travel permits were no longer needed for civilians to enter, travel within, or depart Zone A. Zone B incorporated the Aleutian Islands and that part of the Alaska Peninsula south and west of Becharof Lake below Naknek. Only those civilian workmen with official permits could enter Zone B.

However, civilians in the following categories would not be allowed to enter either Zone A or Zone B without prior military approval: enemy aliens, persons of Japanese ancestry, individuals previously excluded from or denied entry to Alaska for military security reasons, and dependents of Armed Forces personnel.

✫  ✫  ✫

**MEANWHILE, THE ALASKAN DEPARTMENT** had prepared a secret master-deception plan designed especially to excite fresh Japanese specula-tion regarding an American invasion of the Kuriles. Clandestine radio intelligence transmissions enjoyed a measure of success in sup-porting critical deception activities.[9] With this in mind, a portion of the Alaskan Department's plan called for the use of deceptive radio signal traffic to simulate the arrival and presence of new combat-ready forces in the Aleutians. An officer-courier carried the sensitive document to CINCPAC for coordination and then to the Joint Chiefs in Washington for approval. After study, the plan, code-named "Wedlock," was integrated into an overall effort to mislead the Japanese concerning American invasion intentions. It used a renewed threat of American invasion of the Kuriles to persuade the Japanese to relocate additional ground and air forces for the defense of the Kurile Islands rather than to the real American invasion tar-get, which was the Marianas Islands (Guam, Saipan, and Tinian).[10]

In late March 1944, Eleventh Air Force bombers joined the Navy's nocturnal photo-reconnaissance missions to Paramushiro and Shu-mushu. Japanese domestic radio broadcasts again commenced warn-ing that the likelihood of invasion from the north was increasing.[11]

Within a few days, the warning was repeated in greater detail: "We cannot look lightly on our northern front. We must not forget that the men of the army and navy are enduring indescribable hard-ships to complete the defenses of the northern Kuriles. . . . The enemy seems to have decided to increase the pressure on our north-ern front. . . . As the situation in the south becomes acute, the pos-sibility of attack from the north becomes stronger. . . ." The Japanese commentator pointed out that the Americans were looking for even the slightest opening on Japan's defenses to attack from the north, east, and south.[12]

The latest American intelligence data from all sources indicated that the Japanese were expanding and reinforcing their defenses in the Kuriles. Additional airfield building and related construction were being given high priorities.

The War Department order of battle specialists estimated the Japanese troops of all classes currently in the Kuriles to be 40,000.[13]

In late April, Tokyo radio continued to prepare its audience for future air blows that might imperil the Japanese empire. Commentators used the recent nighttime bombings of the Kuriles, only 500 miles from the heart of the Japanese homeland, as an indication of what might be expected later on.[14]

A Japanese document captured on Kwajelein Atoll in the Central Pacific revealed that the Japanese had completed four airfields on Paramushiro and two on Shumushu. According to interpretations of the latest American aerial photographs, the Japanese were believed to have installed some of their latest model radar equipment and anti-aircraft guns to defend their airfields. Previous installations known to have been under construction now appeared to have been finished. The American bomber crews encountered an increase in the number of searchlights and more concentrated anti-aircraft fire. A Soviet observer aboard a Lend-Lease freighter passing through the First Kurile Strait (see Chapter 11) watched a large number of Japanese laborers working along the north coast of Shumushu. Using picks, shovels, and horse-drawn carts, they were digging extensive excavations and long stretches of trenches.[15]

In mid-May, the War Department analysts reported that the Japanese military strength in the Kuriles had increased dramatically, to an estimated 50,000 men. The forces included anti-aircraft units, engineers, communications troops, infantry, special naval landing forces, and field hospital units.[16]

Japanese domestic radio commentators continued to tell people that while the fighting in the South and Central Pacific had recently been very active,

we must not forget to pay attention to our northern frontier. Enemy raids have become quite frequent . . . with the appearance of more than 120 planes in twenty-five raids up to April. . . . The enemy seems to place the main emphasis on reconnaissance rather than bombing. Numerous flares are used for photographs and small bombs are dropped to make us reveal our ground defenses. Not knowing the extent of our defenses, the enemy is using desperate measures to gain that information. . . . If the enemy wants to invade our northern fortress, let them come! No matter how many thousands of troops he may bring, it will end in disaster! Seasoned troops having battle experience in North China and Manchukuo are garrisoned in the fortress. Our air and ground units are not only completely prepared for defense but are full of aggressive spirit.[17]

At the end of May, intelligence analysts confirmed that the Kuriles were being steadily strengthened with more troops and new installations. The War Department revised the estimate of Kurile-based troops upward for a total of 56,000 men.[18]

Within the week, Japanese domestic radio again addressed the vulnerability of the Kuriles:

When General Buckner became head of the Alaskan Department, he stated that sooner or later his American troops must occupy Japanese territory. . . . Various preparations have been made in the Aleutians. The enemy has a powerful air force under command of Maj. General Johnson and a sizeable North Pacific Fleet under Vice-Admiral Fletcher. . . . The enemy has begun lately to attack our northern bases quite frequently. The enemy has large and powerful air bases on Attu, the Semichis, and Amchitka. It is known that large numbers of combat troops in the Aleutians have completed their training. The Aleutians are now the scene of great activity. However, our defenses are completed and secure. We need only to wait for the invasion. . . . The situation is now very tense.[19]

Despite overcast weather in late May and throughout June, Aleutian-based photo-reconnaissance bombers made their predawn missions almost daily over airfields on Paramushiro, Shumushu, and Matsuwa. Six airfields were photographed. Five of the airfields were operational and a total of ninety-three aircraft were visible— seventy-two fighters, twenty bombers, and one transport.[20]

Japanese domestic radio boasted that "due to the accurate shooting of the Japanese anti-aircraft units, the Americans lost two planes during a June 15 raid on the Kuriles. All recent United States raids have been ineffective." American commanders in the Aleutians did not take seriously a Japanese threat of a reprisal raid on Adak Island.[21]

A mid-July domestic radio report from the Kuriles informed the Japanese audience that

> the Japanese troops are all tense over the situation in the Aleutians [where] the American bases are only a few hours flight from the Kuriles. Enemy planes come over daily. Although it angers us, we cannot help saying "even if it is the enemy, it is admirable." . . . Now the air attacks are on a small scale, but soon a large scale bombing attack will begin and the enemy will probably make an invasion, employing hundreds of ships, landing crafts, and sea trucks. On our outposts extending down to Hokkaido from island to island, the troops are on constant alert.[22]

In late July, the War Department analysts issued a new bulletin that reflected a massive increase in the size of the Japanese Kurile defense force. Thirty thousand new troops were believed to have arrived in early June. The total Kurile defenders were now estimated to be 86,000 men.[23]

Using a lengthy recorded report made July 24 on Paramushiro, a Tokyo radio correspondent vividly described the military scene in the northern Kurile area:

> Our defenses are complete! We are ready for any eventuality. . . .
> Our vigilant air-raid lookouts are tormented in the summer by

heavy fog and rain. Not a moment of relaxation. The underground radar plotting room is a scene of exciting action and constant alert. Tonight three enemy planes have been coming in from the east. There go the guns [with] streaks of tracers and bright flowery explosions [from anti-aircraft fire]. There one [plane] goes, wrapped in flames. It explodes! A mid-air disintegration! Another plane plunges down. The remaining plane flees.

According to the narrator, the raiders dropped forty high-explosive bombs, sixty-three incendiaries, and eight flares that caused no damage to the northern Kurile fortress.[24]

A few days later, Tokyo radio described the situation in the northern Kuriles as being acute:

Since the Kiska operation, United States forces in Alaska and the Aleutians have increased a great deal. Several hundred thousand men are stationed throughout the area. . . . These are paratroops, special landing units, and armored units. Half of the Alaskan force is stationed in the Aleutians. . . . During the months of May and June, American bombers, taking advantage of the fogs, attacked the northern Kuriles thirty times and the mid-Kuriles several times.[25]

American interpretation of aerial photographs made in early August revealed that the most strongly defended sections of the northern Kuriles were those on Paramushiro. The main defenses were primarily built around anti-aircraft batteries, although some of the larger guns could have been considered dual-purpose ones. Several covered gun positions and extensive fire trench systems protected the sea approaches and landing beaches.[26]

Information from a Japanese document captured on Saipan disclosed that the Ninety-first Infantry Division was in the Kuriles, where it had absorbed the First Kuriles Garrison. The Forty-third Independent Mixed Brigade was also believed to be in the Kuriles. With the presence of the Ninety-first Division apparently accounting for the recent increase in the size of the defense force, the War Department order of battle estimate of the Kurile troop strength of 86,000 men remained unchanged.[27]

Returning from a visit to the northern Kuriles in late August, a Japanese war correspondent described the conditions there:

> In spite of extreme hardships, the Japanese forces are full of aggressive spirit. The troops are very active in their work and training near the beaches. This scene reminds me of the Yamasaki unit of Attu Island which heroically fought to the last man. . . . Here in the northern Kuriles, persistent enemy air attacks continue. In spite of fog and rain, the impertinent enemy comes over and drops flares and bombs on our troops. There are several islands in the northern Kuriles and ground installations alone are not sufficient against the increasing enemy air attacks. More and more fighters [to oppose the bombers] are urgently needed. . . . After his conference in Honolulu, President Roosevelt came to the Aleutians and for four days, commencing August 3, conferred with Vice-Admiral Fletcher. Later, the president emphasized that . . . in the future there was no worry that Japan would ever menace the Aleutians again. Instead, he said, the Aleutians were the route of attack against the homeland of Japan.[28]

During September, Japanese radio commentators continued to stress the imminence of invasion. Future moves were predicted against the Philippines, the Bonin Islands, and Formosa (Taiwan), with diversionary attacks from the Aleutians against the Kuriles.[29]

Later, in a mood for reminiscence, Tokyo radio reminded its audience that "on August 25 of last year, the withdrawal of our forces from Kiska was announced. On August 29 of that year, the heroic deaths of the entire garrison of Attu Island under the command of Lieutenant General Yamasaki was confirmed. These announcements hit us to very core of our hearts. Now, this August we have heard about the heroic deaths of our forces and fellow Japanese on Saipan."[30]

Intelligence gained from Eleventh Air Force and Fleet Air Wing Four aerial photographs revealed that the Japanese had continued to improve and augment their defensive installations in the Kuriles. Approximately 116 large-caliber anti-aircraft guns were located throughout Paramushiro and Shumushu. The naval air base on Matsuwa was fully developed. A new landing strip was located on Shumushu. With this new facility, the Japanese now had eight known airfields in the northern and mid-Kuriles. Increased defensive activity was noted on Onekotan Island, south of Paramushiro. Stronger fighter opposition and intense anti-aircraft fire were encountered on recent American bombing raids.[31]

For the first time, the Japanese domestic audience was told that the heavy American air raids from the Aleutians were apparently coordinated with other American attacks in the Pacific:

The Americans who have concentrated their forces in the Aleutians have been raiding the northern Kuriles continuously. During the month of September, there were twenty-eight raids with approximately 115 planes. Our air forces intercepted these planes and shot down eight. . . . Furthermore, the enemy in the Aleutians seems to be working in cooperation with the forces in the South Pacific. About September 10, at about the same time that the enemy was making a landing in the Palau Group, they made four continuous raids on the northern Kuriles.[32]

Tokyo strove to rally the domestic audience:

The Japanese soldiers who died on Attu, Gilberts, Marshalls, Saipan, Tinian, and Guam did not die in vain. They inflicted heavy loss of life and materiel upon the enemy America. They died to help defeat that trouble-making people of the world. The United States depended on their tremendous wealth and natural resources. . . . However, material supremacy need not be feared because there is always a limit to material supremacy, and there is no limit on spiritual supremacy which we proudly possess. For example, observe the results accomplished by [Commander] Yainasaki on Attu although he was short of almost everything when the enemy attacked. He has shown the world that we possess spirit, and will never forget it.[33]

G-2 learned that ground defenses in the Kuriles were being extended. Particularly noticeable in recent photographs were additional fire trenches, foxholes, networks of barbed wire, and elaborate anti-tank trenches in areas most vulnerable to amphibious operations as well as areas around the isolated airfields.[34] The latest War Department order of battle bulletin increased the estimated Japanese strength in the Kuriles by 4,000 men, for a total of 90,000.

Bombers returning from missions to the Kuriles reported that fierce fighter defense and anti-aircraft fire, although inaccurate, were very active along the coastlines and in the airfield areas of Paramushiro and Shumushu.[35]

As the battle for the Philippines loomed, the Japanese domestic commentators began paying less attention to the continuing pressure from the Aleutians on the northern Kuriles. However, they reminded their audience that "during October, the enemy raided our northern Kurile positions with a total of 191 planes. Their aims are to cut our line of communications, destroy our ground installations, and inflict as many casualties as possible. For this reason, the enemy has continued to attack [regardless of weather conditions]. The enemy has installed radars and terrain detectors in their planes. With the use of these instruments, it is possible to fly in bad weather and on dark nights."[36]

During November, the Japanese added another 6,000 men to the Kurile Islands' defenses. According to the latest War Department estimates, the islands' total ground force strength reached 96,000 men.[37]

Although the Tokyo radio broadcasts concentrated domestic attention on the battle for the Philippines, where the prospect was for heavy fighting, the commentators did not completely ignore the situation in the north: "[In late November] enemy B-25s and B-24s [approached] Japanese installations on Paramushiro and Shumushu Islands. Sgt. Iwao Naruse, a recent graduate of the Imperial Army Boys Aviation Academy, accounted for one B-24 shot down and one damaged. This engagement was his first experience in aerial combat. Attacking enemy planes caused only slight damage to our installations and were driven away by our defending force."[38]

Beginning in December 1944, Tokyo radio's attention to the threat from the North Pacific abruptly ceased. Instead, throughout the early months of 1945 the domestic radio audience was saturated with running accounts of the rapid squeeze being exerted on Japan's South and Central Pacific defenses. The American "return" to the Philippines was nearing the end. The American flag flew over Iwo Jima. B-29 bombers from the new bases in the Marianas were regularly showering their deadly loads on Japanese cities, especially Tokyo.

In late June 1945, the U.S. Tenth Army completed its conquest of Okinawa on Japan's front door after a long, cruel battle. In the midst of the resulting emergency confusion, Tokyo radio once again felt compelled to address the situation to the north of Japan:

> B-29s flew over our northern island of Hokkaido for the first time on June 27. Any recent activities in the North Pacific thus far have been restricted due to the cold and inclement weather. Nonetheless, enemy movement in the north is becoming intense. On an Aleutian island [Shemya], the enemy is constructing a B-29 air base and the Attu air base has been expanded. These changes indicate that the enemy is waiting for opportunity to attack our homeland from the north. As for the Navy, the powerful 9th (?) Fleet . . . is stationed in the North Pacific at present. There is a submarine base at Sitkin (?) Island. On Amchitka, there is a division of mountain troops.[39]

In July, Tokyo domestic radio used its Japanese-language programs to bolster public morale and inspire a resolve to resist the anticipated enemy attempt to invade the Japanese homeland. The only mention of the Kuriles' vulnerability was on July 22, with a report that "seven enemy warships appeared in the northern waters of the Kurile Islands and shelled the installations on Paramushiro for approximately forty minutes."[40]

After July 22, Tokyo broadcasts ignored the invasion threats from the North Pacific.

**WELL IN ADVANCE OF THE BATTLE** for the Marianas Islands, the American deception activities in the Aleutians, combined with the air and sea harassment of the Kuriles, appeared to have reawakened the Japanese to the threat of an invasion from the north. However, long after Japan had lost the Marianas, the Japanese continued to react to the northern threat. The transfer of more air and ground forces increased steadily for months. As a result, the enemy troop strength in the Kuriles was nearly tripled, and the Eleventh Air Force estimated that one tenth of Japan's air strength had been tied up in the Kuriles.[41]

Meanwhile, stranded behind the security curtain, the frustrated men "somewhere in the Aleutians" had gradually lost hope for any "real" action in the Kuriles. For these men, especially the ground troops, the waiting period for the signal to participate in the war seemed to have no end.

# Chapter Ten

# The Waiting Period in the North Pacific

I N EARLY SPRING OF 1944, four modified B-24s (F-7s) of the Second Photo Charting Squadron arrived to photograph the islands of the Kurile group. The crews and their unique aircraft were first sent to Attu (Casco Cove), where they made familiarization flights in the North Pacific. Then, between June and late August, the job was completed. From the photographs, detailed maps of the Kuriles could be made for strategic-planning purposes. Among other items of interest, the photographs revealed that of the various Japanese airfields and landing strips, there were only three airfields—one each on Shumushu, Paramushiro, and Matsuwa—that were comparable to the major American bases in the Aleutians.

In contrast to the mounting fresh troop concentrations and activities being simulated in the Aleutians by the execution of the modified "Wedlock" deception plan, the actual American military strength in the Aleutians gradually declined. However, sufficient capabilities were available so that Navy surface forces and Army and Navy bombers could conduct their nuisance raids, both day and night, when weather permitted.[1]

Three major military projects continued to keep alive the prospect of future North Pacific offensive operations. One was the establishment of task force staging areas and depot warehousing on Adak;[2] another was the improvement program for three potential

B-29 bomber bases on Adak, Amchitka, and Shemya;[3] and now a third one was the creation and conduct of the Alaskan Department's new North Pacific Combat School (NPCS). Its mission was to orient and prepare the dwindling ground forces in the Aleutians to join any likely Kurile Islands landings.

The Army's Mountain Training Center (MTC) at Camp Hale, Colorado, was the home of the Tenth Mountain Infantry Division that had learned to cope with snow, ice, and other hazards. A portion of the division had already been part of the joint task force assembled for the Kiska assault in 1943.[4] Nearly a year later, in June 1944, the MTC responded to an Alaskan Department request to send a special detachment to Alaska. The detachment's mission was to make a training film that could alert the crews of future crashed aircraft on ways to survive in the subarctic.[5] The detachment of twelve men was already en route to Alaska when the motion picture project was canceled. Instead, on arrival the twelve men were permanently reassigned to the staff of the Alaskan Department's new NPCS, with the expectation that their cold-weather survival expertise could be essential to the school's success.

In August, the NPCS's instructor cadre was assembled on Adak, where ample training areas were available. The school's first class was hastily convened in mid-September to start ten weeks' orientation in mountain and "muskeg" mobility and combat techniques. The graduates of this and subsequent classes would then become their own unit mountaineering instructors.[7] The NPCS faculty and students taught and learned how to survive while enduring the extremes of the Aleutian terrain and weather. An Alaskan Department G-2 survival pamphlet, *Emergency Foods in the Aleutians*,[8] was also available for experimentation.[9] Since the same general terrain and weather conditions found in the Aleutians were prevalent in the Kuriles, the instructors also designed and tested clothing and equipment for use in the North Pacific.[10]

On December 13, the Associated Press released the news of a senior military commanders' meeting at Pearl Harbor. The story immediately stirred fresh speculation regarding the future of the North Pacific invasion route:

> American Army and Navy commanders of the Central Pacific and the Aleutian war areas have just completed a secret conference with Admiral Chester W. Nimitz, Commander of the Pacific Ocean Areas, dealing with future operations against Japan.
>
> Disclosure today of the meetings and names of the participants directed attention toward the Aleutian and Alaskan theaters.
>
> From the North Pacific Front came Lieut. Gen. Delos C. Emmons, commander of the Alaskan Department, and Vice Admiral Frank J. Fletcher, commander in the Aleutians. Lieut. Gen. Simon Bolivar Buckner, Jr., former commander of the Alaskan Department, also attended.
>
> Others at the conference included Admiral Raymond A. Spruance, commander of the United States Fifth Fleet, Vice Admiral C. H. McMorris, Chief of Staff to Admiral Nimitz, and Rear Admiral Forrest P. Sherman, Deputy Chief of Staff in charge of Operations.

By this time, Japan had already commenced its own secret offensive across the North Pacific with the Fu-Go Weapon balloons (Figure 12). The Japanese had recently completed the development of large, hydrogen-filled paper balloons to drift on favorable North Pacific wind currents to the North American continent. In all, over 9,000 Fu-Go Weapon balloons, armed with lethal antipersonnel and incendiary bombs, would be dispatched in the hope of creating panic and forest fires in the United States.

Japan began its campaign by launching 700 balloons in November. Pleased with the initial launching successes, the Japanese then proceeded to send another 8,500 balloons adrift between December 1944 and April 1945. Of the thousands, fewer than 300 balloons were sighted, destroyed, or recovered in the vast area of the United States between the West Coast and the Mississippi River. A few were reported in Canada and along the Mexican border. Meanwhile,

Figure 12. Japanese Fu-Go
Weapon balloon over the North
Pacific near Attu in early April
1945. U.S. Air Force photo.

the Fu-Go intelligence officers waited impatiently throughout December for American reaction to the balloon arrivals. So did Radio Tokyo. On January 4, the Office of Censorship requested newspaper editors and radio broadcasters to give no publicity to balloon incidents. All media in the United States and Alaska adhered to this voluntary censorship. However, because of absence of information regarding the potential danger associated with downed balloons, five children and one woman died on May 5, near Lakeview, Washington, where they encountered balloon wreckage. Finally, on February 17, Radio Tokyo's foreign propaganda broadcasts carried warnings to America by predicting rising balloon casualties and destruction, with something "big" to follow. From America was only silence.[11]

The Aleutians and mainland Alaska were in the path of some of the rudderless balloons. Many incident reports, most of them based on sightings unwitnessed by government officials, were made between January and early April. However, a total of twenty-two incidents were positively confirmed as balloons either destroyed or recovered. In the latter category, the recovery of an undamaged balloon was rare. Most recoveries consisted of debris.

The largest mass destruction of balloons occurred on April 13, when Eleventh Air Force fighters found and gleefully shot down nine of them in the airspace around Attu. At this time in April, multiple sightings were being reported throughout the western Aleutians. Three Soviet Lend-Lease freighters plying the Soviet Far East route reported to have seen three balloons, one of which was downed by gunfire and another, floating on the ocean's surface, was recovered. An American freighter destroyed another floating balloon by gunfire. The last balloon to be recovered in the Aleutians was found floating near Amchitka.

On mainland Alaska, balloon sightings were reported as far north as the Arctic Circle, throughout western Alaska along the Bering Sea coast, and as far east as Cordova. Three balloons were recovered, and debris was found at four other sites, including one on St. Lawrence.[12]

Following the discovery of incendiary devices on the first two balloons recovered in Alaska, federal, territorial, and military fire-control agencies coordinated their emergency plans to cope with forest fires. Alaskan wilderness areas traditionally were most inflammable during the months of May and June.[13]

Although the Japanese had an additional 1,000 balloons ready to launch before the end of April, Tokyo decided to suspend the Fu-Go Weapon campaign. The Japanese sponsors of the project were disappointed by the lack of American attention and reaction; they had no means to measure the effectiveness of the balloons. In addition, the sources for the essential hydrogen gas supply had been bomb-damaged by the rising intensity of the B-29 raids, and the manpower and materials for the necessary repairs were not available.[14]

**THE 100,000 JAPANESE SERVICEMEN** who spent all or part of World War II guarding the Kuriles, like many of the Americans in the Aleutians, eventually decided that they were "forgotten." Far removed from the battles in the South and Central Pacific, they instead fought three different kinds of warfare: one of discomfort with intolerable weather, another of nerves with the Soviet menace in Kamchatka, and a third of uncertainty with the American threat from the Aleutians.

As the American encirclement approached Japan in the spring of 1945, the Kurile outposts were gradually stripped of major units for emergency deployment elsewhere. In the summer, a force of about 25,000 men remained. Most of the stay-behinds were entrenched on the two northern bastions, Paramushiro and Shumushu.[15] The defenders, cut off from their resupply of food and other essentials from the beleaguered homeland, waited for the inevitable assault: Who would attack first? The Americans from the Aleutians? The Soviets from Kamchatka? Or, perhaps, both?

Unlike the Japanese in the Kuriles, the Americans in the Aleutians did not anticipate a serious enemy assault. Nor, after November 1943, did they have the presence of any enemy bomber overhead to make a temporary change in their monotonous lives.

From the time they were sent to the Aleutians, military personnel endured isolation. The men had no choice. By virtue of military need, they came to fill the defense vacuum in the North Pacific. When they did so, they literally disappeared behind the security curtain that separated them from the enemy on the one hand and from the world that they had known on the other. They were not prepared for the inhospitable conditions that they had to face. Instead, they were expected to adjust readily to life in the Aleutians. Some managed to do so. Others did not. Braving harsh weather and spongy tundra, they landed on Umnak and Adak in 1942 and on Amchitka, Attu, and Kiska in 1943.[16] The men were usually occupied with hard labor while hopping island to island. However, they accepted physical exhaustion more readily than they did the growing fear that their continued isolation could also make them indeed the war's "forgotten" men.[17]

Although there was a noticeable upsurge in troop morale immediately following the Attu victory, there were also renewed signs of stress soon afterward. Medical psychiatric case reports noted irritability, inattention, and loss of initiative. Patients who sought scapegoats for their unhappy states of mind openly expressed bitterness toward their military superiors. The number of psychiatric cases due to isolation and monotony continued to rise. Advanced cases required patient evacuation to military hospitals on the West Coast. The Special Services Office of the Alaskan Department, in cooperation with the Red Cross, expanded its programs to combat the spreading malaise. Efforts were made to clarify military rotation policies, outgoing mail delays due to censorship were eased, special entertainment and information programs became available, and Armed Forces radio stations and additional motion picture theaters were eventually established.[18]

BEGINNING IN MID-1943, the Alaska Defense Command (and, later, the Alaskan Department) used the censorship system to obtain postal intelligence. Spot-checking censors extracted pertinent information contained in outgoing mail. Comments and opinions expressed in the letters furnished prime clues for gauging the state of morale among the men in the Aleutians during the 1943–1945 waiting period. Letters from officers, enlisted men, and civilian workmen were selected at random, but the identifications of the writers by name and specific island locations were never disclosed. Month by month, the postal-intelligence analysts continued to report the wavering state of morale throughout the two-year period leading to the climax of the war. A summary of each monthly report and a sampling of typical comments have been extracted to trace the mood of the "forgotten" men of the Aleutians.

### July 1943

The Attu victory proved to be one of the best quick morale boosters of the war. Morale officers reported that it was not the fact that U.S. forces took another island but the news stories of the Attu battle that gave the people at home a new awareness of the soldiers in Alaska. The stories were regarded as delayed tributes to the unsung soldiers who, for many months, carried on their unspectacular warfare against the weather and isolation. The troops had spent many weary months waiting for a break in the seemingly endless monotony. Attu broke that monotony.[19]

### August 1943

A slump in morale was noticeable following the temporary euphoria created by the Attu victory. Military personnel expressed the hope of return to the United States or of transfer to another theater of war. Either opportunity would be welcome. The writers appeared to feel that USO soldiers in the United States received undue consideration for furloughs and promotions. Their comments on certain labor leaders, strikers, and rioters were extremely caustic. They believed that the strikers and rioters at home were violating the very principles of democracy to which the soldiers were committed.

    **Chaplain:** "I had the hardest time getting the men to sing tonight. They were really down in the dumps. . . . Most of them have been here for two years and they have simply given up. These men ought to be reassigned and allowed to return to the States before they go completely nutty."

**Officer:** "Alaska has the strictest censorship in the world."

**Enlisted man:** "No wonder Hitler and Tojo don't have to bomb U.S. industrial plants. John L. Lewis and the hoodlums will close them for the Axis."

**Enlisted man:** "Two more years here and I'd be crazy and so would every one of us who have been here as long as I have. You can't possibly realize what it's like."

**Officer:** "Take everything with a grain of salt so you will not be disappointed later on, for while I anticipate victory, I cannot see an early end of the war."[20]

### September 1943

After the occupation of Kiska, writers made vociferous comments about food, mail, and their fears about their future service. Although the writers were pleased over the success of the American seizure of Kiska and the saving of lives, they also expressed irritation. They resented the fact that some outside troops were brought to the Aleutians for the attack, and they blamed the Navy for permitting the Japanese to escape. Some letter writers referred to the Kiska action as being the ultimate "snipe hunt." Troops were critical of strikes, labor, race riots, and civilian complaints regarding rationing and other restrictions. They felt that they themselves had given their best and expected the people at home to give the same. Morale was not especially low considering the existing conditions. Among the various complaints, censorship continued to be a special target.

**Officer:** "From all reports and news, the home front is certainly messed up."

**Officer:** "Morale is getting noticeably lower by the hour. Everybody is ready to move—either on or back, but nobody is anxious to stay."

**Officer:** "They talk about how wonderful the enlisted men's overseas morale is. Well, all I can say is that they must not have visited here."

**Enlisted man:** "Almost everyone is fed up with everything here. Can't blame us because 15 months on these islands is long enough to drive a guy nuts."

**Officer:** "The monotony is about to drive me crazy. Another winter up here and I will be unfit for human society. Surely they will let me know my rotation status soon. It is 25 months now."

**Officer:** "Censorship seems to be stupid, infantile, inconsistent and . . . moronic."[21]

Even a censor in the Aleutians was troubled by the monotony of

the stuff that I have to read all day long. Do you wonder that it is slowly driving me nuts? However, I picked up a poem today that might explain it somewhat.

The poem reads:

Dear censor,
I hate the thoughts of these tender words
Being read by stranger's eyes
These soul writ words for her alone
These lies and alibis.
So read my letters gently, sir,
They are not meant for you
But for a girl in Arkansas
I write this silly goo.[22]

### October 1943

Lessening tensions and a slight decline in the flood of bitter complaints over everything that touched their lives appeared to have developed. Such indications, however, were not to be construed as meaning that officers and their men were wholly resigned to the situation or were stoically accepting their lengthy tours of duty with the attendant hardships. Additional indications of lowering spirits were reflected in comments concerning slow promotions, the home front's overoptimistic expectations of quick victory, continuing outrage over home front labor strikes and rioting, and the unduly high wages being paid to the defense contractors' civilian workmen.

**Enlisted man:** "They just put us up here and forget us. It's the lost front. Do they ever say anything in the papers about us?"

**Enlisted man:** "Before this war ends I hope I can see a little action, so this is terrible. 30 months in service and no action."

**Enlisted man:** "I am getting so sick and tired of this life we are leading that half the time I wonder if this war is worth the separation and loneliness we have. . . . By the looks of things, they intend to keep us here till we rot."

**Enlisted man:** "All you people think this war will be over soon. The tables may turn on us before it is all over. Just because we win a few battles is no sign that we will win them all."

**Officer:** "These civilian jobs make an Army officer's pay seem like a pittance. We have civilians working here, the lowest getting paid $150 per week. The Army private doing the same work gets $50 a month. Do you get any morale from that?"[23]

### November 1943

A slowdown in complaints was noted during the month as men began to comment more favorably on better food and living conditions. A new rotation policy was not met with much favor because of the two-year minimum service requirement. There was grudging appreciation expressed for the modified censorship regulation that allowed the men to describe their locations as "somewhere in the Aleutians." Although there were still some complaints concerning slow promotions and inactivity, most of the comments were considered to be minor "gripes." After unburdening themselves concerning their hardships, many of the writers appeared to be preoccupied with the overall progress of the war and its aftermath. Labor leaders and strikers were favorite "whipping boys."

**Officer:** "We are now getting fresh food. Morale has hopped up 100 percent. We existed for two months on canned and dehydrated foods."

**Officer:** "We can become eligible for 30 days leave after being up here for 24 months. If we get the leave, it means that we volunteer for another 24 months—so phooey!"

**Officer:** "This life of no action up here is really monotonous. We seem to be as useless here as in the States."

**Officer:** "It's damn discouraging to be sent out of the States as a combat unit and then turn out to be a bunch of stevedores and dock wallopers for three or four months and then, to top it all off, to take over a post that will probably never see action."

**Officer:** "Even though it might tax every one of us to the limit, we must keep powerful armies mobilized throughout the world in order to control the Axis nations—and Russia."[24]

### December 1943

Some improvement in the spirits of military personnel was noted, continuing a slightly upward trend from the low point that occurred shortly after the Kiska operation. The trend was especially noticeable in the far western bases where there was improved housing, fresh food, faster mail service, laundry service, and more entertainment. However, complaints regarding isolated service in the Aleutians were numerous and bitter.

**Officer:** "The worst part of being here is the monotony of everything."

**Officer:** "The soldiers up here are getting pretty much used to the idea that war isn't going to be over tomorrow."

**Officer:** "If I had to choose between hell and the Aleutians, I would take hell any time. There is no land like this in the world."

**Officer:** "I still have another year to go. At times I don't know whether I will still make it or not."

**Enlisted man:** "The conveniences of civilization reach us slowly. However, neither the lack of conveniences nor the weather weigh on us as heavily as nostalgia. It has been two years since most of us has been home."

**Officer:** "Handed out Christmas trees today and you should have seen these fellows! They were tickled pink."[25]

### January 1944

Morale continued to improve, and negative comments were fewer. Interest appeared to be turning from personal problems toward broader and more critical consideration of home front affairs. Strikes engendered a pronounced desire for "revenge" on labor after the war. An almost cynical contempt for anything smacking of politics was expressed. The president's speech of January 11, on the other hand, was well received. What the soldiers seemed to look for primarily in the speech was "encouragement" for an early end to the war and improvement in domestic affairs. Some found such encouragement; others did not.

**Officer:** "If we lose this war (and we could still lose it) it won't be because the armed forces have let down. It will be because those people back there won't back us up."

**Enlisted man:** "Don't tell me that you belong to one of those goddam unions! It certainly is encouraging to get reports from back there that some union has called another strike because they don't think that they are being treated right."

**Officer:** "I'm afraid anybody who has served overseas is going to be violently anti-labor when this is over."

**Officer:** "I thought that the President's speech was swell. Maybe he can wake up some of the people at home so that they will realize that we are engulfed in total war. . . . Can't for the life of me understand some of those people. Does money mean more to them than the lives of men overseas?"

**Enlisted man:** "The President's speech didn't give a great deal of encouragement for the end of the war, but none of us expected that."

**Enlisted man:** "Never have I heard a politician say so little in so many words. Expected him to end up with 'vote for me next election'."[26]

### February 1944

Despite improvement in living conditions and the comforts of civilization, the Aleutian letter writers renewed their chronic voicing of discontent with their inactive lives. However, foremost on their minds continued to be problems on the home front. News of Japanese atrocities on American and Allied prisoners of war was greeted grimly. The lack of promotions and the delay in the new rotation and furlough policies were irksome.

**Officer:** "I hear back in the States they say if the Japs don't treat our prisoners better they're going to do something; might even declare war."

**Officer:** "It's a pity that they didn't release the news of the prisoner atrocities at the time that the coal miners were going to strike."

**Officer:** "I am supposed to teach the GIs to know what they are fighting for and to be willing to die for their country, and back home they aren't willing to give up anything, but just moan and bellyache about everything."

**Officer:** "This inactivity's more horrible than anything else. This island war stinks. I'm developing 'Claustrophobia Islandia'."

**Officer:** "I'd give anything to be on a task force going to the Kurile Islands. Inactivity is the worst enemy a man can have."

**Enlisted man:** "Hell of a place is no name for this place. It's worse than jail."

**Enlisted man:** "Rotation is still in the dream stage, more or less. A few men are gone with the promise of more to follow, but it isn't working as well as it was intended."[27]

**March 1944**

Army and Navy security agents and officers on Adak seized seventy gallons of grain and denatured alcohol and a distillery. Six Army and Navy personnel were arrested. Military authorities hoped that the seizure would stem the clandestine production of poisoned liquor that already resulted in one death. Meanwhile, several civilian workmen at Adak, having broken their contracts with construction companies, complained of unfair treatment subsequent to their discharges. The main complaint was that they were confined in a stockade pending available transportation to the West Coast.[28]

Postal intelligence analysts reported that preoccupation with home front affairs continued as the dominant theme in outgoing mail. No longer did troops dwell on their personal living conditions. The loneliness and boredom in the islands, however, remained a major topic of discussion. The personal conduct of home front civilians was bitterly condemned, mainly because the writers thought that the home front should suffer, too.

**Officer:** "Remember that the people at home are making more money than they ever made before and complain because they can't get the things they never had before."

**Enlisted man:** "I think the best answer yet to those people who say the war will be over soon is, yes, it's all over but the fighting."

**Officer:** "My life in the Aleutians is strictly one of routine and anxiety to get home again. Certainly a more active area would be more interesting, even if dangerous."

**Officer:** "We all need a change. The enlisted men certainly do. They run into one frustration after another."

**Officer:** "The American soldier hates the Jap something awful, and the strikers come next on the list. There is going to be a lot of uprisings and fights between the war-wrecked soldiers and the strikers after this war."[29]

## April 1944

Security officers on Adak thwarted an attempt to smuggle liquor onto the island aboard the SS *Joseph T. Meeks*. Fifty cases of liquor were confiscated.[30]

The trend toward better acceptance of Aleutian service continued to be noticeable, and as a result troop morale appeared to be much higher than it was in the fall of 1943. The principal topic in the outgoing mail still revolved around the endless boredom.

**Enlisted man:** "In two days I will celebrate my second anniversary in this desolate hole. Here I sit and accomplish absolutely nothing."

**Officer:** "I know that there is a war because I saw it in the news reel."

**Enlisted man:** "Promise me that you won't volunteer for overseas. If they ever send you to a place such as this, I know that you will go nuts in a month. But I am lucky. I am already nuts."

**Enlisted man:** "I dream no dreams, I make no plans. I live from day to day with prospective zero, and that is exactly what the Army wants me to do."

**Officer:** "You know it's cold, it's lonely, it's miserable, and every now and then some GI can't take it and blows his top."

**Civilian:** "Military censorship doesn't permit me to mention my specific location. Matter of fact, there is damned little I can write about. However, the regulations are about the same as we had in Trinidad and Bermuda. The only difference here, it's enforced."[31]

## May 1944

Aleutian morale was best described as "normal." Many soldiers and a surprising number of civilians again criticized the inequality of pay given to soldiers and civilians for doing the same work. A few civilians believed that the amount of drinking and gambling was excessive. Although critical of furlough and promotion policies, military personnel appeared to have a better understanding of the situation, but they still did not like the isolation.

**Civilian:** "They work us like hell . . . not like the defense jobs in the States. But that's what we came up here for, I guess. Some of the fellas get to beefing once in a while, and a soldier steps up and says, 'Say, Bud, how much money do you make?' I imagine they feel pretty cheap cause those poor devils here are working for $50 per [month] and have been here for 2 years already and still don't know when they can go home."

**Civilian:** "The soldiers here have to do the same kind of work as the civilians for 1/10 the pay. They work hard, too. They are swell fellas."

**Civilian:** "I am flying airplanes here. Some of the boys are hauling whisky in the planes and haul about 300 cases and get $5 per."

**Civilian:** "Honestly, I have never seen a crazier outfit than this here. . . . I wish the Army would crack down and keep every drop of whisky from coming into camp."

**Air Force officer:** "Can you imagine the boys flying combat for a year without promotion?"

**Officer:** "I want to help prevent some psychiatric accidents among the men at the outposts. These are lonely, very lonely posts and things do occasionally happen. I believe the men will be less likely to crack up if they sincerely think that there is a real necessity that they undergo their ordeals and that good will eventually result from their sacrifices."[32]

### June 1944

An increase in the number of censorship regulation violations in the outer Aleutians was noted. Disciplinary action, including summary courts-martial trial, was being taken.[33]

**THE INVASION OF EUROPE,** the introduction of B-29 bombers over the Japanese homeland, and the increased number of island offensives in the South and Central Pacific had a pronounced effect in the

Aleutians. There was a fresh, brief attitude of optimism. The years of training were over. This was it! However, there were expressed regrets that the Aleutian soldiers had been excluded from participation in history-making events.

**Officer:** "At long last the die is cast in Europe. It makes me feel rather queer up here doing darn little while others are deciding the fate of the nation."

**Officer:** "I imagine everyone at home is pretty excited about the invasion. Well, we up here are, too. Seems as though we are doomed to miss all the excitement, darnit!"

**Enlisted man:** "Just heard that the new B-29 has just bombed the Japanese mainland from bases in China. We have waited a long time for news like that, and it sure feels good."

**Officer:** "Received news of the invasion. I dare say you are bursting with excitement and busy as a bee. You can't imagine our envy, here in this quiet theater."

**Officer:** "The news makes me feel rather useless up here. I had been hoping for a long time that I might finish my time here and be transferred to the European theater before the fight started."

**Officer:** "The food is good, the mail is good, the news is good, everything is good, and I'm good—and lonesome."

**Enlisted man:** "Next month I'll be spending my third birthday in the Aleutians. Monotonous, isn't it?"[34]

### July 1944

Monotony was probably the greatest single contributing factor to the current stagnant level of morale in the Aleutians. Generally, in light of recent developments elsewhere, morale was considered good. However, officers and men alike appeared to feel that their assignments were unimportant and uninteresting when compared with the activity in other theaters of war.

**Officer:** "Today I heard a remark that I think expresses the feelings of everyone here: 'Never have so many been sent so far for so little!'"

**Officer:** "This place isn't bad but the damned monotony gets one down."

**Officer:** "My tour of duty has turned out to be a sentence."

**Enlisted man:** "I use all my ingenuity to kill time when I'm not at work, but still have a lot of it hanging on my hands."

**Enlisted man:** "I have to laugh to see some of the fellows loaf around and then gripe because the war is taking so long to end."[35]

### *August 1944*

Aleutian personnel whose morale appeared to be flagging seemed to be fairly convinced that they were indeed forgotten. The majority watched the development of the war elsewhere with pride and envy while impatiently "sweating out" their own tours of duty. Unimportant work shared the blame for their attitudes. The president's brief visit to the Aleutians was noted but not with interest.

**Chaplain:** "The actual life here is not so hard; it's the idea of being so far from people and home that makes it difficult for them."

**Civilian:** "I'm writing this on Uncle Sam's time, but I haven't anything else that I should be doing."

**Officer:** "Killing time is getting to be my specialty. I'm going to be a bum when this war is over."

**Enlisted man:** "It sure does get monotonous. Always a dull moment."

**Enlisted man:** "Nothing ever happens to me. I just stick in the Aleutians, and stick and stick and stick."

**Enlisted man:** "Talk about being frozen for the duration, I think we're the original icicle that crack was directed at."

**Chaplain:** "Listened to FDR this afternoon. Hope he liked his visit to the Aleutians. Everyone who drops in for 2 or 3 days goes back and says 'not so bad.' Why don't they stay a year? Maybe two years? Then they won't like them so well."[36]

## September 1944

Ironically, the impact of favorable news of American military action and victories in both Europe and the Pacific seemed to crush any hope for improved morale in the Aleutians. The comparison of battle elsewhere with the isolation and inactivity in the Aleutians was too great.

**Officer:** "Isolation with activity isn't bad, or inactivity without isolation can be managed. But the coming winter gives promise of isolation combined with inactivity, and that will be hard to handle."

**Officer:** "Did you read in the paper about Roosevelt's saying that after the war, we are going to have men stationed in the Aleutians? We already knew that up here. It will be us waiting to be rotated or waiting for transportation."

**Enlisted man:** "They talk about a thing called rotation, but I think that they have forgotten us out here in the Aleutians."

**Officer:** "It's deadly dull and I can't see we're serving any useful purpose. The more intelligent seem to be the ones who are the most restless and disgusted; the more placid and unimaginative seem the most content."

**Officer:** "If we force ourselves to be honest, we have little to complain about now, but we still hate the place."

**Officer:** "Gee, but won't I have some thrilling tales of the damned Aleutians after the war. I doubt if we could even give them back to the Aleuts. Of course, I've never seen an Aleut, but he *couldn't* be that stupid."[37]

## October 1944

Entertainment, better food, and added physical comforts were not enough to improve morale in the Aleutians. The ground forces' attitudes, dulled by boredom and inactivity, remained unchanged. Bomber crews, engaged in repeated hazardous missions to the Kuriles, voiced disappointment that they had gone unrecognized and unrewarded.

**Officer:** "He [my commanding officer] has been after me for days to write an article explaining the importance of our presence in the Aleutians, so today I beat my head against a typewriter and ground it out. You see, we have to continually explain these things to the men. Sometimes I wish that someone would take time to explain it to me."

**Air Force officer:** "The majority of the fellows consider it more of an insult than an honor to receive the Air Medal. It's a damn shame that the Eleventh Air Force and the men in it don't get more credit than they do. . . . One of the other crews got the Air Medal after completing twenty-eight missions over the Japanese territory."

**Air Force officer:** "Our work up here will go unnoticed. . . . We'll probably end up with the Air Medal. In Europe, we'd have two Distinguished Flying Crosses by this time."

**Enlisted man:** "I'm okay physically, yet I think my mind is slowly taking a powder on me. Well, maybe it isn't as bad as it sounds, but it's sure getting bad."

**Enlisted man:** "I believe that I told you in my last letter that the topic of Christmas is very painful, especially the prospect of spending a third one on this ghastly volcanic rock."[38]

### November 1944

No improvement in morale was noted. Excellent entertainment and increased physical comforts brought forth enthusiastic and appreciative comments, but they were not enough to overcome the continuing impact of isolation and boredom. Very little new comment appeared regarding the progress of the war, and more resentment was directed to the home front that "doesn't know that there is a war going on."

**Air Force officer:** "You know that we lead a rather dormant life as far as fighter pilots go, and so darned many of the guys in this damned outfit are only too willing to fall into the routine of doing just enough to get by."

**Civilian:** "The Army treats us swell. They are a swell bunch, but they keep them up here too long in this weather."

**Officer:** "We are excellently fed, equipped and housed, but the deadly monotony and lack of constructive activity is bad, especially for officers who should be mentally alert in order to maintain leadership qualities."

**Civilian:** "I think I would be in favor of giving the Aleutians back to Japan and make them live here for punishment."

**Enlisted man:** "Don't know if I'll stand up another year in this isolation, may as well be in the pen, jail in other words, but guess it is all part of this war. Every one must do his part. I sure could do my part somewhere else."[39]

### December 1944 and January 1945

During the holidays, morale appeared to have improved slightly due to excellent motion pictures, USO shows, soldier entertainers, and the distribution of Red Cross Christmas packages. However, the favorable reaction to the holiday celebrations was offset by renewed grumblings concerning rotation and leave policies.

**Officer:** "Went to church Christmas and New Year's. In fact, I haven't missed Mass in several weeks. It gets so lonesome at times. Church is the one thing that connects us with home."

**Officer:** "We didn't have a very nice Christmas. We had a good meal and too much to drink, and that's about all. Morale is not very good, and the proof of that is the number of fights among the men."

**Officer:** "Our Colonel is back in the States on leave and everybody's morale is up 100 percent. He is the one person that we could do without very nicely."

**Officer:** "I get more disgusted with the Army every day. I can't figure the object of everything it does. There are men going back to the States from up here with only 12 months for 60 days in the U.S., and we sit up here with 30 months and don't get out at all."

**Medical officer:** "If I don't lose my marbles first, I should come home a fairly good psychiatrist."[40]

### February 1945

The trend for some improvement in morale as noted last month was continued. Fewer instances of boredom resulting from lack of work were mentioned. However, civilian workmen expressed dissatisfaction with contractors' management. Caustic comments were made regarding the conduct of service schools at Aleutian posts. The rotation and leave policies as well as the lack of promotions suffered never-ending criticism.

**Civilian:** "This outfit is all foremen. And paid for it. Nobody to do the work. Did you ever hear of bulldozer foreman or oiler foreman? I never did either. Padded payroll is my idea of this outfit. Wonder why the Army doesn't put a stop to them?"

**Officer:** "I have to put on a school for other officers on field fortifications, mines, obstacles, etc. Can you feature a utilities man teaching combat engineering?"

**Officer:** "We are really in the middle of red tape. I am going to artillery school two nights a week. Then I take an infantry school three nights a week, and then officers call on Saturday."

**Officer:** "Only have to go to school two nights a week instead of five. They changed the time so we could have three in the afternoon, which isn't so bad."

**Officer:** "Being a captain for three years while slobs like [deleted] are promoted over me has definitely ended my love for the military service."

**Air Force officer:** "This is a poor theater for flying officers to get promotions. Some of the second lieutenants have been in grade a year longer than I have. One kid got his promotion to first [lieutenant] a short while back after being a second lieutenant for thirty-two months."

**Air Force officer:** "We have now completed our twenty-third mission. . . . Beginning to believe that I'm going to join the huge army of permanent second lieutenants. The Aleutians are full of them."

**Officer:** "The leave and rotation situation is still pretty much in the air. No matter how we figure, there will be very few lucky enough to get a 30-day leave."[41]

### March 1945

The slight upward trend in morale was maintained. However, critical remarks continued to be made concerning the military training programs being conducted at various Aleutian stations. Both officers and men seemed to regard them as a waste of time.

**Officer:** "This infantry school I'm now attending is absolutely a farce."

**Officer:** "What am I studying in school? Nothing, but I'm supposed to be studying weapons and tactics, a little communications, and a lot of bunk."

**Officer:** "Needless to say, our work up here is not too important in the whole setup and I sort of wonder if it isn't an awful waste of personnel and money. But I guess somebody thinks it is OK."[42]

### April 1945

Although the content of outgoing mail indicated that morale continued to show slight improvement, the service schools that were being conducted in the Aleutians continued to be roundly ridiculed. Both officers and men seemed to feel that these schools were too repetitious and served no useful purpose. There was praise for the living conditions. Shock was expressed following the news of President Roosevelt's death.

**Officer:** "We are getting snowed under with work every day. If they keep interrupting us with training, firing range, etc., we'll never get caught up."

**Officer:** "Next week we play war and take the battalion out in the field. Shall probably get to sleep in the tundra or something."

**Officer:** "We are going to a six-weeks school here and don't enjoy it at all. . . . Got a four-hour hike on snowshoes coming soon and lots of silly stuff."

**Air Force officer:** "We listen to the news from the States each evening and heard the activities of our mighty Eleventh Air Force—the forgotten Air Force—mentioned twice last week. That's a lot of publicity for us."

**Air Force officer:** "Maybe someone will wake up to the fact that we are fighting a war up here and give us a little publicity someday. We deserve some credit for flying over water that you can live in only twenty minutes if forced down."

**Civilian:** "This is the day that President Roosevelt died. I'm glad that he lived to see victory was near in Europe and inevitable in Asia."[43]

### May 1945

No discernible change in morale had developed. The isolated Aleutian soldiers speculated that they would be "sidelined" during the worldwide military personnel readjustment period following the end of the war in Europe. The point system for discharge eligibility was roundly criticized as being unfair because of the high point value assigned to dependent children. Such a policy, Aleutian soldiers believed, allowed recently inducted men to be discharged for parenthood credits, while many married men, having served long periods of time overseas, had no opportunity to secure parenthood credits.

**Enlisted man:** "It was unusual to notice the extreme calmness with which the men up here received the VE day news. I guess that they're all thinking that this will affect their possibilities of rotation adversely."

**Enlisted man:** "The boys were disappointed with the Army demobilization plan's point system. Of all the men up here with four years or more in the Army, only a few are certain to get out."

**Enlisted man:** "The news of the discharges has had such a profound effect here that the silence is appalling. So few are eligible for it inside of a year or so. Rather suppose that most of the men are here for the duration."[44]

### June 1945

A decided drop in Aleutian morale was evident. A primary factor for the decline was individual reaction to the War Department troop readjustment program ("the point system") and the cancellation of rotation prospects. As a result, censors recorded caustic and vitriolic comments. Most writers apparently concluded that the Aleutians had become, more than ever, the forgotten theater of war and no provisions had been made for the relief of "tundra-happy" soldiers.

**Officer:** "Had to laugh the other day. A directive came out relative to leaves and furloughs, and it had virtually frozen them. A paragraph at the end of it stated that morale must be kept at the usual high standard."

**Enlisted man:** "This point system might look all right on paper, but they have it set too high and don't give enough credit for our being in this dump."

**Enlisted man:** "The morale at this post has sunk to a new low. Rotation is frozen and so are furloughs, they say."

**Officer:** "This damned place is intolerable enough. These cockeyed censorship regulations add insult to injury."

**Air Force officer:** "The men up here don't get promotions until it is time to go home after 35 missions or 400 combat hours. Awards . . . are held in abeyance until the crew are ready to go home; consequently, when VE day was declared and the point system went into effect, all of us were shy about 20 points."[45]

### July 1945

Morale changed little. Men in the Aleutians again turned their attention inward to assess their own situation as U.S. forces elsewhere began to concentrate on the planned invasion of Japan. Any notion that they might participate in the invasion via the Kuriles now seemed too remote to be seriously considered.

**Officer:** "This may sound unpatriotic, but most of the men have been up here for more than two years and they are fed up with soldiering. Their patriotism has all been used up. They feel that they are the forgotten men."

**Officer:** "I hope some guys still possess the fire and zeal that prosecution of this war requires, because I don't anymore. I hope the guys who decided to keep us up here for two years also had the foresight to write us off the books as completely valueless after those two years are up."

**Civilian:** "I will be glad when it is over. Never again in a place like this. It is like being in jail. I don't see how the soldiers stand it without going crazy."[46]

### August 1–14, 1945

The world-shaking events that developed one after the other in the Far East did little to stem the ebbing morale in the Aleutians.

**Civilian:** "Sure has been good news this week with the atomic bomb and the news of Russia declaring war on the Japs. It should not take long before it is all over."

**Officer:** "Of course, the big news is the peace offer by the Japanese. When will I be able to get to you and home?"

**Officer:** "I want to do only that which is necessary and to be left alone until they are ready to let me go. I am willing to quit any time."

**Enlisted man:** "My morale is at its lowest right now. . . . The way things look, we have been left here to rot. Someone is giving us a raw deal."[47]

✮ ✮ ✮

**UNKNOWN TO THE JAPANESE,** any prospect for an American decision to invade the Kuriles from the Aleutians was fading in early 1945. As a neutral country in the war with Japan, the Soviet Union had cast its shadow on the North Pacific well beyond the Kamchatka Peninsula. Soviet ships carrying Lend-Lease cargoes from the West Coast to the Soviet Far East for years plied the North Pacific among both the Aleutian and Kurile Islands.

Now, with the Soviet Union's entry in the war on August 8, 1945, and Japan's surrender a week later, the long waiting period in the Aleutians had ended at last for the many who had waited in vain.

*Chapter Eleven*

# Soviet Presence in the North Pacific

**A**FTER THE UNITED STATES agreed to provide Lend-Lease arms, equipment, raw materials, and food to the Soviet Union in 1941, the first question was obvious: Where were the ships to deliver the urgent Lend-Lease items to the embattled Red Army? The Soviet Union's merchant marine fleet was so depleted that it could provide only a small portion of the cargo fleet that would be needed. However, despite a world shortage of Allied vessels in 1941–42, the United States and Great Britain strove to find additional ships to begin the flow of massive aid to the desperate Soviets.

Then, assuming that Allied shipyards eventually would provide new ships to fill the void, the next question also became obvious: Which ocean routes could be used to reach Soviet or Soviet-friendly ports? In the early efforts to meet delivery schedules, three main Lend-Lease sea routes were first developed: north, Persian Gulf, and Soviet Far East.

The north (Russian) route from the Atlantic through the Barents Sea to the Soviet ports of Murmanak and Archangel was the shortest, but its use proved to be extremely dangerous. German bombers, submarines, and surface warships hounded the Lend-Lease supply convoys, so much so that use of the route had to be suspended several times during the war. Of the 760 ships that sailed the route, 96 were sunk.[1]

The Persian Gulf route from the South Atlantic around Africa to Iraqi and Iranian ports was the longest and safest, but there were many initial obstacles to overcome. Although the early cargo ships were bulging with vital supplies when they arrived at the ports, the overland delivery of the cargoes became only a trickle. The port management and facilities were inadequate. The neglected highways and railroads from the ports across Iran to the Soviet Union's borders were unreliable. Eventually, by 1943, American military engineers successfully modernized the ports and Iranian transportation arteries. Thereafter, the volume of Lend-Lease deliveries to the Soviet Union via the Persian Gulf route showed vast improvement.[2]

**A THIRD MAJOR DELIVERY ROUTE,** a potentially dangerous one via the North Pacific to the Soviet Far East, was by far the busiest and most productive. A total of 9,233,280 tons of supplies, or 47 percent of all Lend-Lease aid to the Soviet Union, was delivered to eastern Siberian ports.[3]

Since the late eighteenth century, Japan and Russia had been perennial adversaries in the Far East, yet they discovered common advantages in dampening their animosity in 1941. On April 13, months before Germany invaded the Soviet Union and Japan attacked Pearl Harbor, the Soviet Union and Japan signed a neutrality treaty. Honoring the pact, the Soviets remained neutral in the Pacific war until April 5, 1945 (see Chapter 12). The neutrality pact served the Soviet Union well, especially in one respect. It established the basis for an agreement by the Japanese to allow, albeit grudgingly, Soviet ships with Lend-Lease cargoes from the West Coast to pass through Japanese-controlled waters.

While it gave the Soviet Union much better access to aid, the Soviet Far East route also had several disadvantages: (1) the Japanese agreement limited the cargoes to nonarmament items such as industrial and railroad equipment, trucks, raw materials, petroleum products, and food; (2) once unloaded in the Far East, most cargoes would be reloaded on the Soviets' underequipped railroad trains and then moved thousands of miles across Siberia; and (3) the allocation of Soviet ships from the scant Soviet merchant marine fleet would be insufficient to transport the mounting Lend-Lease supplies being stockpiled on the West Coast.[4] The United States designated the ports of Tacoma, Washington, and Portland, Oregon, to handle the Lend-Lease export shipments. (Later, when the Tacoma and Portland facilities became overwhelmed, excess Lend-Lease supplies were diverted to San Francisco and Seattle for exporting.)

Vladivostok was the principal Soviet port of destination for the Soviet Far East route. Just as the delivery program was being organized in 1941, Japan struck at Pearl Harbor. Any plans for using American flagships were immediately dropped. With the United States and Japan at war, all cargoes bound for Vladivostok thereafter would be carried only on vessels flying the Soviet flag.[5]

In January 1942, the first four Soviet freighters sailed for Vladivostok.[6] During the spring and as summer approached, the few available Soviet flagships made only slight use of the run from the West Coast to the Soviet Far East over the great circle route that crossed the North Pacific via the Aleutian Islands. When the Japanese struck at the Aleutians in June 1942, the United States realized that any further advancement of the Japanese from Kiska and Attu could have serious consequences for the future operation of the vital Lend-Lease supply route.[7]

During this time, American aid to the Soviet Union was falling far behind the promised schedules, not only over the Soviet Far East route but also over the north and Persian Gulf routes. To increase the supply flow from the West Coast ports, the Soviet Union asked for the Lend-Lease transfer of twenty cargo ships to be used in the Pacific under Soviet registry and manned by Soviet crews. However, because American troops and arms were being rushed to counter the Japanese in the South Pacific, the United States was unable to fulfill the request at that time.[8]

Fortunately, American shipyards began launching new vessels at an amazing rate. In November 1942, fifty-three Lend-Lease cargo freighters and six tankers were formally transferred to Soviet flag registry for service on the Soviet Far East route.[9]

Throughout the war, the cargo ships and tankers that began their voyages on the Soviet Far East route from the West Coast ports made their first landfall as they neared the eastern end of the Aleutian Islands chain. They sought and entered Unimak Pass, where the established sea lane went from the North Pacific to the Bering Sea. Unimak Pass was situated between Unimak Island on the east and Akutan and Unalaska (Dutch Harbor) Islands on the west.

Some of the Soviet ships occasionally anchored at Akutan or Dutch Harbor for fuel, repairs, or other emergencies. Accidents occurred, such as the one reported in April 1944, when an unexplained explosion sank the USSR *Pavlin Vinogradov* as it approached Unimak Pass. From a crew of forty-five, nine survivors were rescued. The USSR brought them to Akutan. Later, six of them were removed to Dutch Harbor for further medical treatment.[10]

From Unimak Pass, the ships continued their great circle voyages in a shallow arc across the Bering Sea not far below the Soviet Union's Komandorskiy Islands. Their next landfall was Cape Lopatka, at the lower tip of Kamchatka. Here they approached the First Kurile Strait and came in contact with the Japanese.

The narrow First Kurile Strait separated the Soviet Kamchatka from the shores of Japan's northern-most Kurile island of Shumushu. One half of the strait was considered to be Soviet waters, and the other half Japanese. Unfortunately, a broad reef prevented large vessels from navigating on the Kamchatka side. The Soviet Lend-Lease ships therefore had to pass through Japanese waters for the first time.[11]

Like threading the eye of a needle, the Soviet vessels negotiated the narrow strait and entered the Sea of Okhotsk. Here the Soviets, uneasy about the Japanese sensitivity to the Soviet use of American Lend-Lease vessels, split the route into two segments. The vessels of original Soviet merchant marine registry sailed to the southwest and entered the Sea of Japan through the La Perouse Strait. The Lend-Lease vessels that now carried the Soviet flag and registry proceeded across the Sea of Okhotsk to the north end of Sakhalin Island. They entered the long Tatar Strait between the island and the Asian mainland.

The destination of most of the vessels was Vladivostok and its satellite port of Nakhodka. However, the Soviet decision to send vessels via the Tatar Strait allowed some cargoes to be off-loaded at the port of Nikolayevsk at the mouth of the Amur River and even up the river at Komsomol'sk. In addition, other cargoes were landed on either side of the Tatar Strait at Aleksandrovak (Sakhalin) and Sovet-skaya Gavan.

Vladivostok was not prepared to handle the cargoes of the early supply-laden ships. The port lacked cranes, piers, and sufficient rail-road cars. Vladivostok, like the initial Persian Gulf ports, became a bottleneck. Ships rode at anchor while waiting for unloading berths. Barges were used to remove some of the cargoes, which then were stockpiled on the shore. In the confusion, the stockpiles became ready targets for pilferage. The situation, however, commenced to improve in late 1942 when the United States provided giant unloading cranes and railroad equipment. The Soviet NKVD reduced the amount of pilfering by closer supervision of the port's stevedores.[12]

In the early stages of the war, while Tokyo was concerned about the fate of the Japanese garrisons in the Aleutians, the parade of Soviet freighters began to increase through the Kuriles. Japanese navy patrols became openly aggressive in intercepting, searching, and detaining Soviet ships whose cargoes were suspected to contain armaments. In August 1943, having evacuated the Japanese garrison from Kiska, Tokyo was acutely aware of the increasing American military strength in the Pacific as well as the Red Army's successes on the German front. Tokyo was in no mood to risk sparking a military confrontation with the Soviet Union and forbade any further harassment of the Soviet ships.[13] During the war, however, Japanese submarines sank nine Soviet ships, apparently by mistake.[14]

Waterfront gossip on the West Coast loading docks fanned numerous rumors concerning Japanese-Soviet high-seas confrontations in the Sea of Okhotsk and the Sea of Japan. One such unsubstantiated rumor reached and was circulated in southeast Alaska during the 1943 fishing season. The rumor claimed that Soviet freighters had been seen in Japanese ports. Their cargoes of American-made Lend-Lease trucks were alleged to have been seized (even though motor vehicles were not on the Japanese taboo list).[15]

After the first group of Lend-Lease vessels was released to Soviet registry, the number of American-made Soviet flag-bearing ships was later more than doubled to a total of 125.[16] Freed of routine Japanese harassment, the Lend-Lease ships manned by Soviet crews began delivering record tonnages to the Soviet Far East.[17]

Following the Japanese evacuation of Kiska, American Army and Navy aircraft intensified their search of North Pacific and Bering Sea areas for fresh signs of enemy activity. The aerial patrols reported the sighting of Soviet freighters in increasing numbers. Although the Soviets had agreed to a recognition system of American challenge and Soviet response, not all of the Soviet vessels complied. In the absence of any recognition responses, the ships were identified by their Soviet flags or by Soviet insignia painted on their superstructures.

The surge in shipping activity on the Soviet Far East route was reflected in the number of Soviet ship sightings reported during the final five months of 1943:

August—eight freighters and one tanker
September—nine freighters
October—thirty-five freighters and two tankers
November—twenty-three freighters and one tanker
December—twenty-six freighters. During the period of December
    11–18, high winds, heavy seas, and generally adverse weather

prevailed in the areas west of the Aleutians. The hull of the sea-battered freighter *Valeriy Chkalov* split amidships and sank.[18] Total—101 freighters and four tankers[19]

**NOT ALL OF THE SOVIET SHIPS** that were loaded on the West Coast were destined to pass through Japanese waters. After entering the Bering Sea, some of them arrived at Petropavlovsk with supplies to bolster the stockpiles of the Soviet Union's major military bastion on Kamchatka. Most of the supply ships that were switched from the Soviet Far East route at midpoint carried their cargoes northward through the Bering Strait on the Soviet Arctic route.[20]

The Soviet Union's urgent need for aircraft led to early negotiations to establish an Alaska-Siberia air ferry route to deliver Lend-Lease fighters and bombers to the German front. Beginning in October 1942, the first factory-new airplanes that had been flown to Fairbanks, Alaska, were released to Red air force pilots. From Alaska, Soviet airmen began to shuttle nearly 8,000 aircraft across the vast Siberian wilderness. The ferry route operated without major interruptions during the war. The successful deliveries were made possible by a series of Siberian relay air bases located at Uel'kal, Seymchan, Yakutsk, Kirensk, and then Krasnoyarsk, where the route terminated at its juncture with the Trans-Siberian Railroad.

The Soviet Arctic route for ships was created with a major mission of delivering supplies to the Lend-Lease ferry air bases in Siberia. The shipping route was used primarily during the summer months of 1943, 1944, and 1945. After entering the Arctic Ocean from the Bering Sea via the Bering Strait, the supply ships turned westward to reach the Arctic coast ports at the mouths of north-flowing Siberian rivers, including the Kolyma, Lena, Yenisey, and Ob. The unloaded cargoes were then transshipped on smaller craft and barges up the rivers as far as possible. The vital supplies were hauled overland to the air bases or to the Trans-Siberian Railroad for further distribution.[21]

In addition to the thousands of Lend-Lease fighters, bombers, and transports flown from Alaska across Siberia, the Soviets also ferried thirty Lend-Lease PBY-type flying boats from Kodiak Island across the Bering Sea to Magadan, Siberia, in the late summer of 1944.[22]

The Soviet Arctic route was used to deliver 452,000 tons of Lend-Lease cargoes, or approximately 3 percent of the total Lend-Lease aid to the Soviet Union.[23] When the Soviet Arctic route tonnage was added to the Soviet Far East route's massive deliveries, however, 50 percent of all American waterborne aid reached the Soviet Union via the North Pacific.

WHEN THE LEND-LEASE TRANSFERS of cargo ships and tankers were made, the Soviets provided the merchant marine crews to man them. However, when a major Lend-Lease naval ship transfer program was initiated in early 1945, the personnel situation was much more complex. The operating crews of the naval craft would require special training, which the United States Navy agreed to undertake. The overall program called for the Lend-Lease of 556 ships ranging from frigates down to various smaller craft.[24]

The Navy Department decided that some of the warships should be transferred and their crews trained at a North Pacific location. The vacant facilities at Fort Randall on Cold Bay at the end of the Alaska Peninsula were selected to be used by the Navy's project, code-named "Hula-Two." Beginning in February 1945, the Navy had two months to prepare for the arrival of the first 2,000 Soviet naval trainees. By mid-April, the training program was in full swing. At regularly scheduled intervals, training group followed training group. When each group completed its familiarization cruises with its respective warships, the vessels themselves were formally transferred to the Soviet navy.

In all, twenty-eight frigates, thirty-two subchasers, fifty-five minesweepers, thirty infantry landing craft, and four floating repair craft became additions to the Soviet navy. As the end of the war approached, flotillas of the Lend-Lease warships, manned by 12,400 Hula-Two trained crewmen, sailed from Cold Bay to Petropavlovsk and other Soviet Far East ports.[25]

**THE SECURITY CURTAIN HAD SHELTERED** the 1942–1945 Soviet presence in the North Pacific. With the war reaching its climax and the Soviets preparing to occupy the Kurile Islands, the time was coming when the security curtain in the North Pacific would no longer be needed and would be lifted.

*Chapter Twelve*

# Lifting the Security Curtain

**A**S 1945 DAWNED, the security curtain masking the mood and activity in the Aleutians' Zone B remained in effect. The established military rules of censorship continued to be rigidly enforced among the troops and civilian workmen alike. Army counterintelligence agents promptly investigated all attempted violations. At the same time, the Alaskan Department's public relations officers maintained surveillance over the output of a handful of war correspondents.

In Alaska's Zone A, the regulations governing the censorship of all military personal mail were likewise unchanged. In contrast, the Office of Censorship, having concluded that it was virtually impossible for the enemy to intercept mail and cable channels from Alaska, decided to cease the examination of civilian mail and cables. However, the monitoring of radiotelegraph and telephone circuits continued. In addition, the Office of Censorship expected Alaska's newspaper editors and radio broadcasters to observe as usual the provisions of the two Codes of Wartime Practices.[1]

Meanwhile, in early February 1945, the Big Three leaders assembled at Yalta for a decisive meeting. Here, Stalin confirmed that the Soviet Union would join the Allies against Japan ninety days from the date of Germany's anticipated collapse and surrender.[2] Stalin planned, in coordination with the Chinese, to drive the Japanese army from Manchuria and northern China. Roosevelt and his advisors endorsed Stalin's stated objectives. They wanted the Red Army's offensive to prevent the Japanese Kwantung Army from being withdrawn from Manchuria to bolster the Japanese home islands' defenses. Stalin, in turn, wanted to regain the rights and territories in Manchuria and Sakhalin Island that Russia surrendered to Japan in the 1905 Treaty of Portsmouth. In addition, Stalin sought to regain territorial possession of the Kurile Islands that Russia had ceded to Japan in the 1875 Treaty of Commerce and Navigation. Roosevelt raised no objection to Stalin's territorial expectations.[4]

Two months after the Yalta summit meeting, on April 5, the Soviet Union denounced the 1941 Soviet-Japanese Neutrality Treaty. The denunciation should have warned Japan that the Red Army was being readied to move in the Far East. However, Soviet foreign minister Molotov wanted to keep the Soviet Far East Lend-Lease route to Vladivostok open as long as possible. Using skilled diplomatic skullduggery, Molotov privately convinced Tokyo that the treaty, although denounced, would remain in effect until 1946.[5]

With the battle for Okinawa in Japan's front door now under way in April, American forces were being gathered for the assault on Japan itself. Plans for the landings on southern Kyushu were being readied. Deception specialists hoped to make the Tokyo high command believe that the attempt to invade Japan could come from some other point. In the north, the threat from the Aleutians would be strengthened with newspaper stories that airborne units were being trained in the northern United States for possible use from Alaska. Before the Soviet entry and the war's abrupt end in August, Washington strategists in reality were considering the movement of airborne forces to Alaska in the hope that the Japanese defense forces in the Kuriles and Hokkaido would be kept in place instead of being transferred to Kyushu.[6]

Anticipating that the hard-fought conquest of Kyushu would be successful, American planners already looked ahead to the climactic invasion of the Japanese heartland—Honshu itself. Among other deception operations, the fiction of Aleutian military reinforcements would be continued to play on enemy fears. False radio traffic would be circulated to and between fictional U.S. units in the Aleutians, dummy bases would be built there for fictional divisions, and dyed markers to indicate points of invasion from the north would be dropped on Hokkaido's beaches. (In addition, because Japan was concerned that the Soviet Union would enter the war, Tokyo should be convinced that a Soviet invasion threat to the Kurile Islands still existed.[7])

Between May and July, Red Army troops from the European front were moved to the Soviet Far East. They were placed to conduct an overwhelming campaign against the Japanese defenders in Manchuria, Korea, southern Sakhalin, and the Kuriles. By early August, over a million men were in position. If the lightning offensive went according to plan, Red Army and Navy units then would enter Sakhalin and land on the Kuriles.[8]

After the Soviets entered the war on August 8, the Red Army's carefully planned assault to crush the Kwantung Army was launched the next morning. For nearly a week thereafter, there were no indications of a similar assault on the Kuriles. Instead, following the dramatic Japanese unconditional surrender on August 15, the defenders of the Kuriles expected the arrival of an American occupation force, which the Japanese did not intend to resist.[9]

Unlike the Red Army's orchestrated thrust through Manchuria, the Soviet plan for the seizure of the Kuriles seemed to have been made in haste. On August 18, three days after Japan's surrender, a fleet of sixty miscellaneous vessels, including fifteen Lend-Lease infantry landing craft recently arrived from Cold Bay,[10] was assembled and sailed from Petropavlovsk with troops, armed sailors, and NKVD border-guard personnel. Concealed by fog, the fleet arrived at its destination, Shumushu and Paramushiro. Since the war was over, the Soviets did not expect resistance, but they were surprised by the Japanese defiance. The disorganized fighting was sometimes savage for five days, after which the Japanese surrendered and were disarmed on August 23.

The Soviet occupation of the remainder of the Kurile Islands was less violent and was completed on September 4.[11]

Fog and persistent cloudiness prevented the Eleventh Air Force from observing the extent of the early Soviet occupation of the Kuriles. However, on August 23, four B-24 bombers succeeded in making photographs of the northern islands. Throughout the final week of August, similar photographic missions were attempted but hindered by weather.

On September 4, two B-24s again approached the Kuriles but, for the first time, Soviet fighters interfered. The American bombers were turned back.[12] After completing 1,500 sorties to the Kuriles in 1943–1945, the Eleventh Air Force had flown its last Kuriles mission of the war.

On September 20, 1945, the Soviet Union declared the Kurile Islands to be Soviet territory.

Effective October 1, the commanding general of the Alaskan Department issued Public Proclamation No. 11, which removed all remaining wartime security restrictions in mainland Alaska and the Aleutian Islands.[13] The American security curtain in the North Pacific was now officially lifted. In its stead, with the coming of the Cold War, another curtain between the Aleutians and the Kuriles would be lowered. Under the control of the Soviet Union, this curtain would prove to be an iron one.

# Conclusion

**O**BSCURED BY THE WAR-LONG SECURITY CURTAIN in the North Pacific, American forces in the Aleutians had waited restlessly for the opportunity to fulfill any planned invasion of the Kuriles en route to Japan. On Adak, the staging facilities and warehousing for a 50,000-man invasion task force were completed during the 1943–1945 waiting period. However, in spring 1945, the accelerated American victories in the Central and South Pacific were allowing American forces to approach ever closer to Japan. At the same time, the Yalta summit agreement to bring the Soviet Union into the war was changing the overall strategy for the conduct of the war. As a result, the Joint Chiefs of Staff no longer entertained any serious notion of an invasion of Japan from the north. Any invasion preparations from the Aleutians now came to naught.

It might once have been feasible for Aleutian-based troops to have landed in the Kuriles at the same time that the American-planned invasion of Kyushu was undertaken. However, with the use of the atomic bomb and the entry of the Soviet Union in the war, the decisive August 1945 events came swiftly, one after the other, with no hope for the involvement of the idle Aleutian troops. Without even a last-minute role in sharing the occupation of the Kuriles with the Soviets, the disillusioned Aleutian veterans were denied any substantive historical recognition for their potential usefulness when the last North Pacific hidden war ended.

On September 2, world attention was focused on the pageantry being presented in Tokyo Bay on the decks of the battleship *Missouri* marking the defeat of Japan. The climactic ceremonies, however, did not foresee that, although the need for the wartime North Pacific security curtain would no longer exist, the shadows of frustrated American servicemen would linger indefinitely in the Aleutians.

# Postscript

**B** EGINNING IN 1944, some of the evicted Japanese-American residents of Alaska were allowed to return to their Alaskan homes. Others followed after the Alaskan Department removed all wartime restrictions on them. Harry Kawabe chose to make his postwar home in Seattle. Here he became a widely recognized and influential leader in the Japanese-American community. He occasionally visited Seward to oversee his properties there and to award scholarships to worthy Alaskan students. He died in Seattle in 1969 and his wife, Tomo, died in 1970.[1]

After Taeko Tatsuguchi was notified in Japan of the death of her husband, Dr. Paul Tatsuguchi, on Attu in 1943, she and her two daughters somehow managed to survive during the war on a small widow's pension. After the arrival of the American occupation forces, she found employment with them. In 1954, Taeko and her children went to Hawaii, where she commenced a career as an English-Japanese translator. When mother and daughters became naturalized American citizens, the older daughter, Misako, adopted the name Joy, and Mutsuko the name Laura. Taeko, Joy, and Laura moved to California, where, inspired by her father's example, Joy enrolled in Pacific Union College to study nursing; Laura followed a year later. Laura, like her father, also attended Loma Linda University. Joy married SDA elder Takashi Shiraishi, who became Health and temperance secretary for the Japan Union Conference in Tokyo. Laura, a registered nurse, married California businessman Joel Davis. Taeko had four grandchildren, Joy's two in Japan, and Laura's twins.[2]

During the conduct of the two hidden wars in the North Pacific, the Japanese captured twenty-six American prisoners of war. Although three of the captured men died en route to Japan, the others were successfully repatriated soon after Japan's surrender.

The Navy provided thirteen of the prisoners captured during the Japanese raid on Dutch Harbor and the enemy's subsequent occupation of Kiska. Three were airmen defending Dutch Harbor, and the remaining ten were the weathermen on Kiska. Of the latter, nine were promptly sent to Japan. The tenth man, W. C. House, after evading capture for several weeks, was also sent to Japan. Until repatriated in 1945, House did not know what had become of the other nine men, and the men incorrectly assumed that House had died on Kiska.

After Dutch Harbor, no further Navy airmen fell into Japanese hands, but the Navy did provide the Japanese with two crewmen from the submarine *S-44*. On patrol near the Kurile Islands during the night of October 7, 1943, the *S-44* made contact with what was thought to be an enemy freighter. The submarine surfaced to shell it. Unfortunately, the target was a charging Japanese destroyer. Deadly gunfire sank the *S-44*, leaving several men in the water. The destroyer's searchlight beam located two of the men, R.M. 3rd Class William P. Whitmore and C.T.M. Ernest A. Duva, and rescued them. The two men were taken first to Paramushiro for interrogation, then to Japan.[3]

Seven of the eight repatriated Eleventh Air Force airmen were listed as missing in action during their captivity. The Eleventh Air Force insisted that the enemy claim to have captured the eighth prisoner, S. Sgt. Francis L. McEowen, was a hoax. Although listed as killed in action, McEowen was released in 1945, became a career engineer, and died thirty-six years later of a heart ailment in Indianapolis, Indiana.[4]

Every one of the 175 Eleventh Air Force airmen and the sixty-seven Fleet Air Wing Four flyers interned for months in Siberia by the Soviet Union were able to "escape" after being sworn to secrecy.

They kept the secret for over forty years, until 1988. Congress was persuaded to pass legislation that reclassified their secret status so that they were qualified for Veterans Administration disability compensation and other benefits to which former prisoners of war were entitled.[5] In 1992, the Department of the Air Force, and later the Department of the Navy, officially redesignated the wartime status of the 242 internees as prisoners of war.

The forty remaining Aleuts from Attu were placed in a Japanese internment camp on Hokkaido in 1942. During the next three years, death among the Aleuts would become commonplace due to illness and lack of food. Forty percent would die. Three babies born in Japan also would die. As a result, only twenty-four Aleuts and one infant born in Japan would manage to survive. They were identified in six interrelated family groups: (1) Sergi Artomonoff; (2) Olean H., Elizabeth, Gregory, Nickolas, John, Innokinty, Willie, Julia P., and Mary T. L. Golodoff; (3) John, Annie Y., Martha, Marina, Angelina, and Stephen Hodikoff; (4) Mike and Parascovia H. Lokanin; (5) Alfred and Alfred, Jr. (born in Japan) Prokipioff; and (6) Elizabeth, Alexai M., Agnes, and Fekle Prossoff. Released at war's end, they were eager to return to their home on Attu. A cruel disappointment awaited them. Attu was now littered with battle debris. Once the Aleuts were convinced that Attu was forever denied to them, some of the broken-hearted Attu islanders decided to join other Aleuts in a resettlement colony on Atka Island instead.[6]

Following the formalities of the Japanese surrender on September 2, the Soviets then insisted that the recently established American weather stations at Khabarovsk and Petropavlovsk must be removed. The Navy argued that the new weather services would be of value during the occupation of Japan and the two installations therefore should remain in Siberia. Whereupon the Soviet placed so many restrictions on the American operations that they became ineffective. Finally, by mutual Soviet-American agreement, both stations ceased their activities on December 15, 1945, and the Americans and their equipment were soon evacuated.[7]

# Nisei MIS Roster[1]

1. Ashizawa, Roy
2. Furuiye, Nobuo
3. Hayashida, George
4. Higashi, Yumiji
5. Hotta, Yoshio
6. Imon, Frank
7. Ishida, Ted
8. Ito, Shigeo
9. Kanagaki, Hiroshi
10. Kariya, Juetts
11. Kawakami, Jake
12. Kawasaki, Dick
13. Kobata, George
14. Kuroiwa, Mickey
15. Mayeda, Charles
16. Mayeda, Masami
17. Miyata, Roy
18. Morita, Yoshio
19. Moriwaki, Ben
20. Muto, George
21. Nakamura, Howard
22. Nakao, Pete
23. Nishikawa, William
24. Nishimura, Harold
25. Noguchi, Ted
26. Oda, Dick
27. Ogawa, Tadashi
28. Oka, Chikara Don
29. Otsuka, Frank
30. Shibata, Mitsuru
31. Sugimoto, Sam
32. Sugimoto, Toshiro
33. Suyehiro, Hideo Henry
34. Tanakatsubo, Satsuki
35. Tsukiji, George
36. Tsurutani, James
37. Umetani, Yasuo Sam
38. Wada, Hiroma William
39. Yagi, Steve
40. Yamada, Tetsuji

## Appendix B

# Propaganda Leaflets

**IN THE EUROPEAN WAR,** Americans had a measure of success in the use of propaganda leaflets to induce German and Italian combat troops to surrender. Given the Japanese bushido indoctrination and cultural background, the American call for Japanese surrender was having little effect.

Instead, "morale" leaflets were being introduced in the Pacific war, including the Aleutian campaign. Morale leaflets did not call for any immediate action. Rather, they strove to induce a general state of depression by repeated reminders of hopeless situations, such as those on Attu and Kiska.

The Eleventh Air Force bombers frequently mixed leaflets with the bombs they dropped on Kiska after August 1942. Later, when the Japanese reoccupied Attu, bombers delivered small quantities of leaflets there also.[1]

Leaflets were produced in various shapes, sizes, and colors. One such leaflet had the shape, size, and color of the Japanese *kiri* leaf (Figure 13). A short message on one side of the leaflet, referring to mythology, reminded superstitious Japanese that "before spring comes a second time, American bombs, like kiri leaves falling far away, will bring sadness and misfortune." The leaflet was first intended for the Doolittle raiders to drop over Tokyo in April 1942, but was never used.[2]

Figure 13. "Before spring comes a second time, American bombs, like kiri leaves falling far away, will bring sadness and misfortune." G-2 ADC files.

Another one of the leaflets contained the fading silhouette of a Japanese warship and an outline map of Attu Island (Figure 14). Copies were used during the Attu blockade in the early spring of 1943. The leaflet contained a taunting message: "Attu! Where has the Imperial Navy gone?"

A third leaflet was one that, in retrospect, might have been an embarrassment to the Americans. On one side of the leaflet was a simple map of the North Pacific between Japan and Alaska, with the island of Kiska highlighted (Figure 15). On the leaflet's reverse side was a long message informing the Japanese on Kiska that "you have been forsaken. There is no hope of reinforcement."[3] Throughout early August 1943, tens of thousands of leaflets were showered on Kiska. It was true that the Japanese were not reinforced. Instead, they were long gone, rescued in late July by a Japanese evacuation fleet without American knowledge.

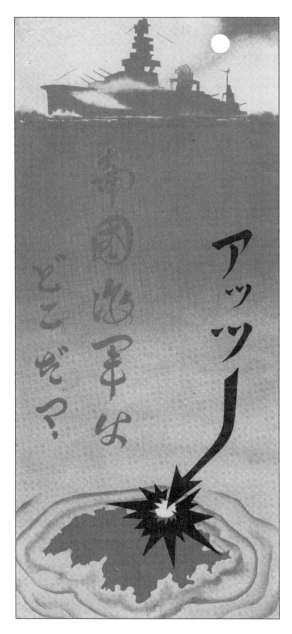

Figure 14. "Attu! Where has the Imperial Navy gone?" (Message on
reverse side.) G-2 ADC files.

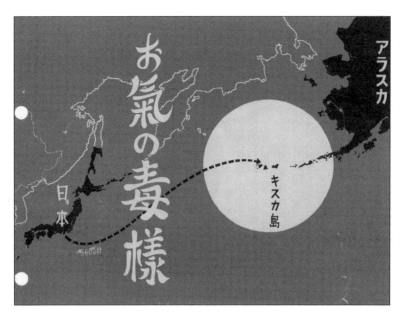

Figure 15. "You have been forsaken. There is no hope of reinforcement." (Message on reverse side.) G-2 ADC files.

# Tatsuguchi Diary Translation

**S**EVERAL EARLY VERSIONS of the Tatsuguchi diary's English-language translation existed before the original diary in Tatsuguchi's Japanese handwriting disappeared. What did Paul Tatsuguchi actually write? Nobody is certain of the answer.

The translation appended below[1] contains a multitude of garbled words, obvious typographical errors, and misinformation. The text is reproduced here exactly as it appeared in the original. The garbles and errors may have been those of typists who made hasty copies of the original translation. The misinformation regarding the continuing Attu battle beyond his field hospital probably was Tatsuguchi's interpretation of Japanese hearsay. The original translator of this version of the diary is unknown.

### Diary of Nobuo Tatsuguchi
### Northern 5216 Detachment
### North Seas Defense Field Hospital (Attu, Alaska) May 12th [1943]

Carrier based plane flew over. We opened fire at it. There is a low fog and the summit clear. Evacuated to the summit. Air raids carried out frequently. Heard loud noise, it is naval gunfire. Prepared battle equipment.

### May 13th Battle

The U.S. Forces landed at Shiba Dai and Massacre Bay. The enemy advanced to the bottom Misuna Yame, Shiba Dai—north end of Attu Island. Have engaged them on the other hand. Massacre Bay is defended by only one platoon but upon the unexpected attack the machine cannon was destroyed and we have withdrawn at night. We have captured 20 enemy rifles. There is tremendous mountain gun-fighting. About 15 patients came in the field hospital. The field hospital is situated by the Area Engineers Unit.

### May 14th Battle

Our two submarines from Kiska Island assisting us have greatly damaged two enemy ships. 1st Lt. Sukuki died by shots from rifle. Continuous flow of wounded soldiers came into the field hospital. In the enemy the U.S. Forces used gas but no damage was done on account of strong wind. Took refuge in the trenches in the daytime and took care of the wounded during the bombardment. The enemy strength must be a division. Our desperate defense is holding out.

### May 15th Battle

Continuous flow of wounded to our field hospital caused by the fierce bombardment of enemy land and naval forces. The enemy has a great number of Negroes and Indians. The West Arm Unit have withdrawn to near Shitagata-Dai in a raid. I was ordered to the West Arm but it was called off. Just lay down from fatigue in the barracks. Facial expressions of the soldiers back from the West Arm is tense. They all went back to the firing line soon.

### May 16th Battle

If Shitagata-Dai is taken by the enemy the fate of East Army is decided, so orders was given to destroy all the wounded soldiers by giving them shots in the arm and die painless. At the last minute there was an order from Headquarters Sector Units to proceed to Chichagof Harbor by way of Umnose. At one o'clock in the morning wounded soldiers from infantry was lost so accompanied the patients there. Was on air raid, so we took refuge in the former field hospital cave. The guns of the enemy were roaring continuously.

### May 17th Battle

At night about 11:30 o'clock under cover of darkness I left the cave. Walked over muddy roads and steep hills of no-man's land. No matter how far or how much we went we did not get over the pass. Was rather irritated in the fog by the thought of getting lost. Sat down after 30–40 steps would sleep dream and wake up, same thing over again. We had few wounded and had to carry them on stretchers. They got frost-bitten feet, did not move after all the effort. Met Sector Commander Colonel Jamaki. The pass is a straight line without any width and steep line toward Chichagof Harbor. Sitting on the rear and lifting the feet I slid down very smoothly and changed direction with the sword. Lay down about 20 minutes after that, went down to Chichagof Harbor. After struggling all the time, had expended nine hours, for all this without leaving any patients. Opened a new field hospital. Walking now is extremely difficult. The results of our navy, the submarines and aerial underwater craft in this vicinity of Chichagof Harbor since the 14th, sank battleships, cruisers, 31 destroyer transports of airborne troops and 6 other transport ships. By the favorable turn of battle on the East Arm reserves came back off shore Shiba Dai. Five destroyers are guarding 2 transport ships.

### May 18th Battle

The Yenagawa Detachment abandoned East Arm and withdrew to Umanose. About 60 wounded came to the hospital. I had to care for them myself through the night. Everybody made combat preparations and waited. Had two grenades ready. 2nd Lt. Omrechft from the front line and Hokuokin Yama, said farewell. At night a patient came in, he had engaged a friendly unit by mistake and who had received a wound on the wrist. His counter sign is Isahi Hoke.

### May 19th Battle

At night there is a phone call from Sector Unit Quarters, in some spots of the beach there are some friendly fleet-type planes waiting. Went into the village church—felt like home, someone's home. Some blankets were scattered around. Was told to answer a field order presumed to have been dropped by an enemy officer in Massacre Bay. Was ordered to evaluate a detail map sketch of Massacre and Holtz Bay in possession of Captain Robert Edward, Adjutant of Colonel Smith, got tired and went to sleep. 1st Lt. Uglie is also in charge of translation.

### May 20th Battle

The hard fighting of our 303rd Battalion in Massacre Bay is fierce and it is to our advantage. Have captured enemy weapons and used that to fight enemy closing under fog. Five our men and one medical NCO died. Heard that enemy pilots dropped several bombs near Omanose. The enemy naval gun-firing near our hospital is fierce, stopping about 30 yards away.

### May 21st Battle

Was strafed when amputating a patient's arm. It is the first time since moving to Chicagof Harbor that I went into an air raid shelter. Enemy plane is a Martin Arvousness. Our Company Commander is severe and he has said his last word to his men and officers, that he will die tomorrow. Gave all his articles away. Everyone that heard this became desperate and things became disorderly. Hasty chap this fellow. Officers on the front are doing a fine job.

## May 22nd Battle

Air raid again. Straffing killed one medical man. Medical man Reyki wounded, a fractured arm during the night. A mortar came awful close.

## May 23rd Battle

Seventeen friendly medium bombers destroyed a cruiser off shore. By naval gun fire a hit was scored on the pillar pole of tents for patients and the tents gave in and killed two instantly. From 2 o'clock in the morning to 6 o'clock stayed in the fox holes. No food for 2 days.

## May 24th Battle

It sleeted and was extremely cold. Stayed in Misumi barracks alone. A great amount of shells were dropped by naval fire. Rocks and mud flew all around. The roof fell down. In a fox hole five yards away, Hayaske, a medical man, died instantly by a penetration of shell fire through his heart.

## May 25th Battle

Naval gun-firing, aerial bombardment, trench warfare, the worst yet to come. The enemy is constructing positions. Our commander was killed at Umanose. They cannot fully accommodate all the patients. It has been said that at Massacre Bay district the road coming to Sector Unit Headquarters has been isolated.

## May 26th Battle

By naval gunfiring it felt like Misumi barracks blew up and things shook up tremendously. Consciousness became vague. One tent burned down from a hit by an incendiary bomb. Straffing planes hit the next room. Two hits from a fifty machine gun. One stopped on the ceiling, the other penetrated my room. Looks like an awful mess from the sand and pebbles that came from the roof. Mirose, 1st Lt., from Medical Corps is also wounded bad. There was a ceremony of granting of the Imperial Edict. The last line of Umanose was broken through. No hope for reinforcements. We will die for cause of Imperial Edict.

### May 27th Battle

Diarrhea broke out and continues steady, pains severe. Took everything in pills, morphine and opium, then everybody slept well. Straffing by planes. Roof broke through. There is less than 700 left from more than 3500 troops wounded from coast defense units. Field hospital held post office, the rest are on the firing line.

### May 28th Battle

The remaining ration is for 2 days. Our artillery has been completely destroyed. There is sound of trench mortar, also AA guns. The company on the bottom of Attu Iuju has been completely annihilated except for one or two. 303rd Company has been defeated. Yenegawa is still holding. Umanose continues cases of suicides. Half of Sector Unit Headquarters has been blown away. Heard they have 400 shots of morphine to wounded to kill them. Ate half dried thistle it is the first time I have eaten something fresh in months, it was a delicacy. Order from the Sector Unit Commander to move hospital to the Island but it was called off.

### May 29th Battle

Today at 2 o'clock we assembled at Headquarters, the field hospital took also part. The last assault is to be carried out. All the patients in the hospital were made to commit suicide. I am only 33 years old and I am to die. Have no regrets. Bonsei to the Emperor. I am grateful that I have kept the peace in my soul which Enkist [Christ] bestowed on me at 8 o'clock. I took care of all patients with a grenade. Goodby Iaeke [Taeko], my beloved wife, who loved me to the last. Until we meet again grant you God-speed Misaka [Misako], who just became four years old, will grow up unhindered. If I feel sorry for you Takiko [Mutsuko] born February this year and gone before without seeing your father. Well goodbye Mitsue, Brothers Hocan, Sukoshan, Masachan, Mitichan, goodbye. The number participating in this attack is a little over a thousand. Will try to take enemy artillery position. It seems the enemy will probably make an all out attack tomorrow.

## History

| | |
|---|---|
| March 16, 1919 | Graduated from Kerjie Middle School, Hira Shima |
| March 2, 1923 | Graduated from Travier English Academy |
| September 15, 1926 to May 22, 1932 | Medical Department, Pacific Union College, Angwin, California |
| September 1933 to June 1937 | College of Medical Evangelists |
| September 8, 1938 | Received California medical license |
| January 10, 1941 | Inducted First Imperial Guard Infantry (Japan) |
| January 13, 1941 | Joined First Imperial Guard Infantry (Japan) |
| May 1, 1941 | Ordered as officer candidate |
| August 1, 1941 | Promoted to corporal |
| September 1941 | Entered Army Medical School |
| October 24, 1941 | Graduated |
| October 31, 1941 | Promoted to sergeant major; ordered probationary officer |
| December 1, 1941 | Acting officer |

*Appendix D*

# Signal Intelligence Operations

**A**FTER WORLD WAR I, the use and protection of electronic communications, especially radiotelegraphy, were rapidly refined. As the clouds of World War II approached, government officials and military commanders were dependent on the far-flung instant communication that radiotelegraphy provided. To safeguard the content of secret messages, intricate codes were devised and frequently changed.

Signal intelligence agencies were challenged to extract information from the coded communications of potential or real enemies. In the United States, the Army and Navy met the challenge early by adopting similar signal intelligence analytical systems. The Army's organization became known as the Signal Intelligence Service (ancestor of the Army Security Agency), and the Navy's was the Communications Security Unit (OP-20-G). Using intercept and direction-finder stations, traffic analysts fixed the locations of transmitting stations, whether land-based or at sea, and studied the volume and pattern of the messages to determine the possible intentions of the enemy. Skilled cryptoanalysts engaged in the tedious process of code-breaking so that the content of intercepted messages in their original texts could be read. The development of American code-breaking expertise was first dramatically demonstrated on the eve of the battle for Midway and Dutch Harbor in

Figure 16. Radio intelligence direction finder station on Attu, 1943. Photo courtesy Irving Payne.

1942. Rigid security measures were enforced to protect the highly secret successful code-breaking from becoming known.[1]

**IN THE RUSH TO PROVIDE CRUCIAL SUPPORT** to the developing Aleutian campaign, the 102nd Signal Radio Intelligence Company[2] arrived at Anchorage on September 11, 1942. Within a month, an official directive assigned the unit to cover all Japanese radio circuits within monitoring range.[3] Priority was given to continuous coverage of the enemy's Aleutian radio net circuits.

Direction finder and additional intercept stations eventually were located at Fairbanks, Nome, Cold Bay, Adak, and Amchitka. After the seizure of Attu and Kiska, stations were also placed there (Figures 16 and 17). Better coverage of the Japanese radio frequency bands was obtained at night, when the enemy wireless traffic was

Figure 17. Radio intelligence installation, Murder Point, Attu. Photo courtesy Irving Payne.

heaviest. Consequently, more station operators were on night shifts than on day watches.[4]

Meanwhile, Lt. Irving P. Payne arrived at Adak to organize the Alaska Intelligence Center (AIC) (Figures 18 and 19). To this signal intelligence center later flowed intercepted radio traffic and direction finder bearings not only from Alaskan stations but from West Coast and Hawaiian stations as well. The fresh intelligence produced from combined traffic analyses, direction bearings, and code-breaking was reported promptly to the Adak advance headquarters of the Alaska Defense Command and the North Pacific Fleet.[5]

On May 29, 1943, having already anticipated the completed seizure of Attu, Army and Navy commanders prepared a joint plan for an amphibious task force (ATF-9) to capture Kiska promptly. They sent the plan through CINCPAC to the Joint Chiefs of Staff for consideration. Three weeks later, the plan was approved, with an assault target date of August 15.[6]

Figure 18. Alaska Intelligence Center (AIC) on Adak, winter of 1942–1943. Photo courtesy Irving Payne.

Figure 19. Operations room, Alaska Intelligence Center on Adak, where intercepted Japanese radio traffic was broken and translated. Direction finder bearings also were plotted. Photo courtesy Irving Payne.

However, on July 9, Lieutenant Payne at Adak's AIC reported that current analysis of intercepted enemy message traffic seemed to indicate that the Japanese had reached a decision to evacuate the Kiska garrison.[7] On the following day, Kiska radio transmissions in the northern Japanese radio net abruptly became increasingly active. Kiska radio sent a surge of high-priority messages to Otaru (Hokkaido) and Tokyo. At the same time, flurries of operational messages continued to be sent between Paramushiro and Sapporo (Hokkaido).[8]

Throughout the period from July 17 to July 24, Kiska radio remained unusually busy, with most of the communications destined for Sapporo. Intercepted radio traffic indicated that the Japanese considered an American landing assault on Kiska to be imminent. In view of the heavy aerial bombardment and the Navy's blockade of the island, G-2 intelligence analysts concluded that the Kiska defense force could not repulse an amphibious landing without additional Japanese troops and naval support. Therefore, prompt enemy reinforcement of Kiska appeared to be the most likely Japanese action.

Adverse weather conditions hampered the air and surface search for an enemy naval force reported to be west of the Aleutians. Surface contact had not yet been made on July 24. However, Kiska radio again became exceptionally active, with thirty-six high-priority messages, eighteen to Sapporo, ten to Tokyo, and eight to Paramushiro. Following a slack period between July 25 and July 27, Kiska radio again sent urgent traffic to Sapporo and Paramushiro during the morning hours of July 28.

On July 29, radio intercept stations reported Kiska radio to be inactive. However, the current G-2 study of enemy capabilities assumed that Japanese surface forces were still present in the North Pacific area and that such forces were within striking distance of the western Aleutians.[10]

When Vice Admiral Kinkaid gathered the ATF-9 commanders at Adak in late July to complete the final details for the landings, they were confronted with incomplete radio traffic reports of Japanese activity. In brief, the lack of complete reports indicated at least an enemy withdrawal from the Kiska beaches to the island's highlands. Or, even more importantly, the entire Kiska garrison might have been evacuated. These indications, coupled with several unsolved ATF-9 problems, prompted Vice Admiral Kinkaid to ask CINCPAC for a postponement of D-Day. CINCPAC declined because, in view of the North Pacific naval blockade, an enemy evacuation of the Kiska garrison could not be readily assumed. The Kiska assault therefore would proceed as scheduled.[11]

Kiska radio remained inactive throughout the first week of August. Its usual frequencies were not heard. Analysts speculated that recent American air raids and naval bombardments might have damaged the Kiska radio station. G-2 cautioned that the intervals of foggy, overcast weather were affording the unmolested enemy time and opportunity for preparing Kiska's defenses.[12] Kiska radio continued to be inactive during the second week of August. Meanwhile, American bombers intensified their pre-invasion strikes on Kiska. On August 14, G-2 noted that the enemy anti-aircraft fire capability for resisting aerial bombardment appeared to have been removed.[13]

In accordance with the August 15 D-Day schedule, Allied troops landed on Kiska. A thorough search confirmed that the enemy had indeed evacuated the island in late July.

DURING THE KURILE WAITING PERIOD OF THE WAR, the Alaska signal radio intelligence stations reached their peak performance. In November 1944, the direction-finder net established a new operational record by handling a total of 1,547 messages during the month. Special recognition also was given to the traffic-analysis team, whose predictions of enemy intentions grew in direct proportion to the continuing heavy volume of intercepted messages and direction finder hearings.[14] Fifty years later, Colonel Payne, recalling his role with the signal radio intelligence unit in Alaska, wrote: "Our main responsibility was to keep all concerned of any and all movements or plans that the Japanese might make. And I believe that we did a real good job of it!"[15]

# Endnotes

## Preface

1. Donald M. Goldstein and Katherine V. Dillon (eds.), *Fading Victory: The Diary of Admiral Matome Ugaki, 1941–1945* (Pittsburgh: University of Pittsburgh Press, 1991), 137; John H. Cloe, *The Aleutian Warriors,* Part I (Missoula, Mont.: Pictorial Histories Publishing, 1990), 86.

2. Alaska Defense Command/Alaskan Department G-2 Weekly Periodic Reports, together with annexes 3 (psychological), 4 (counterintelligence), and 6 (air information) thereto, May 1943–September 1945, Record Group 338, National Archives (hereafter cited as G-2 Report number, annex number, and date).

## Introduction

1. Buckner soon was promoted to major general, then lieutenant general.

2. Fourth Army's area of responsibility included the fledgling Alaska Defense Command on its north flank. With the coming of war, the Western Defense Command was then established and combined with the Fourth Army to consolidate the Army's defenses on the Pacific coastline.

3. Fourth Army letter, General DeWitt to Governor Gruening (information copy to General Buckner), August 6, 1941.

4. The Thirteenth Naval District had responsibility for the Pacific Ocean area adjacent to Alaska.

5. Otis Hays, Jr., "When War Came to Seward," *Alaska Journal* (Autumn, 1983), 110.

6. Brian Garfield, *The Thousand-Mile War* (Fairbanks: University of Alaska Press, 1995), 80.

## 1. Lowering the Security Curtain

1. Theodore F. Koop, *Weapon of Silence* (Chicago: University of Chicago Press, 1946), 20.

2. Ibid., 21.

3. Frank Luther Mott, *American Journalism* (New York: Macmillan, 1950), 761–62.

4. Ibid., 763–64.

5. Koop, *Weapon of Silence*, 46.

6. Otis Hays, Jr., "The Silent Years in Alaska," *Alaska Journal* (1986 anthology), 143.

7. Koop, *Weapon of Silence*, 261.

8. Hays, "The Silent Years in Alaska," 143.

9. Koop, *Weapon of Silence*, 262.

10. Ronald K. Inouye, "Harry Sotaro Kawabe: Issei Businessman of Seward and Seattle," *Alaska History* (Spring, 1990), 35–36.

11. Hays, "When War Came to Seward," 107. Because of Alaska's dependence on the exposed port at Seward, an alternate marine-rail connection was built to the port of Whittier on Prince William Sound, and the construction of the overland Alaska Highway was undertaken. After the war, Seward never regained its earlier prominence.

12. G-2 Report no. 146, annex 4, March 10, 1945. Civilian custodians were appointed to manage Kawabe's business enterprises during the war. Among Kawabe's personal property was an heirloom set of samurai swords, which also were placed in custodial care.

13. Hays, "When War Came to Seward," 112.

14. Alaska Defense Command Public Proclamation No. 1, April 7, 1942.

15. G-2 Report no. 146, annex 4, March 10, 1945.

## 2. Confrontation in the Aleutians

1. Kevin Don Hutchison, *World War II in the North Pacific* (Westport, Conn.: Greenwood Press, 1994), 197. The other nine members were Radioman 3rd Class R. Christiansen, Chief Pharmacy Mate R. L. Coffield, Radioman 3rd Class M. L. Courtney, Radioman 2nd Class L. L. Eckles, Aerographers Mate 2nd Class W. I. Gaffney, Cook 3rd Class J. C. McCandless, Seaman 1st Class G. T. Palmer, Aerographers Mate 2nd Class J. L. Turner, and Aerographers Mate 3rd Class W. M. Winfrey.

2. Norman E. Rourke, *War Comes to Alaska: The Dutch Harbor Attack, June 3–4, 1942* (Shippensburg, Pa.: White Mane Publishing Co., 1997), 26–28.

3. Stan Cohen, *The Forgotten War,* Volume Two (Missoula, Mont.: Pictorial Histories Publishing, 1988), 211.

4. Garfield, *The Thousand-Mile War,* 116n; Dean Kohlhoff, *When the Wind Was a River: Aleut Evacuation in World War II* (Seattle: University of Washington Press, 1995), 63–72, 77–81.

5. Domei press release, "Kiska Report," Tokyo, August 1942.

6. Cohen, *The Forgotten War,* Volume Two, 211; Ethel Ross Oliver, *Journal of an Aleutian Year* (Seattle: University of Washington Press, 1998), 254; W. M. Winfrey letter to author, October 14, 1996. The only survivor of the Navy weather station remaining on Kiska was the detachment's canine mascot, Explosion. The dog was found among the abandoned Japanese canine pets after the enemy evacuated Kiska a year later, in 1943. After the war, Winfrey learned that a member of the U.S. task force on Kiska adopted Explosion.

7. Donald M. Goldstein and Katherine V. Dillon, *The Williwaw War* (Fayetteville: University of Arkansas Press, 1992), 235–36.

8. Lt. Col. William J. Verbeck, acting Alaska Defense Command G-2, statement to author, September 1943. Verbeck was a fluent Japanese linguist and a recognized specialist on Japanese culture.

9. Alaska Defense Command Public Proclamation No. 4, June 30, 1942.

10. Hays, "The Silent Years in Alaska," 143.

11. Robert W. Desmond, *Tides of War: World News Reporting, 1931–1945* (Iowa City: University of Iowa Press, 1984), 252. Among the correspondents were Keith Wheeler, *Chicago Times*; Sherman Montrose, NEA-Acme Newspictures; Frank H. Bartholomew, United Press vice president in charge of the Pacific area; Russell Annabel and James A. McLean, both of United Press; Eugene Burns and William L. Worden, both of Associated Press; Clarence Hamm, Associated Press Photos; Howard Handleman, International News Service; Foster Hailey, *New York Times*; Robert Sherrod, *Time*; Charles Perryman, *News of the Day* cameraman; Morley Cassidy, *Philadelphia Bulletin*; John Tresilian, *New York Daily News* photographer; William Gilman, North American Newspaper Alliance; and Wilson Foster, National Broadcasting Company.

12. Hays, "The Silent Years in Alaska," 143.

13. William Gilman, *Our Hidden Front* (New York: Reynal & Hitchcock, 1944), 114.

14. Garfield, *The Thousand-Mile War,* 237–38; Cloe, *The Aleutian Warriors,* 231.

### 3. The Secret Nisei in the Aleutian Campaign

1. Associated Press release, Washington, D.C., December 23, 1994.

2. Lyn Crost, *Honor by Fire: Japanese Americans at War in Europe and the Pacific* (Novato, Calif.: Presidio Press, 1994), 21–25.

3. Otis Hays, Jr., *The Alaska-Siberia Connection: The World War II Air Route* (College Station: Texas A&M University Press, 1996), 63.

4. Frank Imon letter to author, August 15, 1996.

5. Pete Nakao letter to author, August 24, 1996.

## 4. Nisei Support at Attu and Kiska

1. John Prados, *Combined Fleet Decoded: The Secret History of American Intelligence and the Japanese Navy in World War II* (New York: Random House, 1995), 495–96.

2. G-2 Report no. 100, annex 3, April 22, 1944; G-2 Report no. 106, annex 3, June 3, 1944. Radio Tokyo's domestic broadcasts continued to insist that the Attu defenders numbered 2,900, not the 2,400 that the Americans estimated. The defending force also included navy personnel and civilians.

3. Pete Nakao letter to author, August 24, 1996.

4. Frank Imon letter to author, August 15, 1996.

5. Gilman, *Our Hidden Front,* 216–17; Joseph D. Harrington, *Yankee Samurai: The Secret Role of Nisei in America's Pacific Victory* (Detroit: Pettigrew Enterprises, 1979), 102.

6. Pete Nakao letter to author, August 24, 1996. In 1996, fifty-three years after the battle on Attu, Pete Nakao at his Arleta, California, home received a telephone call from Harold Peterson, who was living in Port Angeles, Washington. Peterson's son had found Nakao's telephone number through an Internet search. Nakao began to make plans for visiting Peterson. Before Nakao could commence his sentimental trip, Peterson's wife notified him that her husband had died while undergoing surgery.

7. Harrington, *Yankee Samurai,* 101.

8. G-2 Report no. 60, July 7, 1943.

9. G-2 Report no. 66, August 28, 1943.

10. G-2 Report no. 68, September 11, 1943.

11. Gerhard L. Weinberg, *A World at Arms* (New York: Cambridge University Press, 1994), 497.

12. Radio Tokyo's frequent praise for Yamasaki through 1944 usually identified him by his Attu rank of colonel, not his posthumous rank of general.

13. G-2 Report no. 100, annex 3, April 22, 1944.

14. G-2 Report no. 106, annex 3, June 3, 1944.

15. Chikara Don Oka letter to author, June 9, 1996.

16. Nubuo Furuiye letter to author, July 10, 1996.

17. Frank Imon letter to author, August 15, 1996.

18. Harrington, *Yankee Samurai*, 110.

19. G-2 Reports no. 67, annex 4, August 7, 1943, and no. 75, annex 4, October 30, 1943.

20. At war's end, Wada was the interpreter for Adm. Thomas C. Kinkaid when he accepted the surrender of Japanese forces in Korea.

21. The JICPOA Annex was located near downtown Honolulu. Nisei were not permitted at the main JICPOA in Pearl Harbor without Caucasian escort.

22. Nobuo Furuiye letter to author, July 10, 1996; Harrington, *Yankee Samurai*, 128, 148, 163, 199, 201.

23. Chikara Don Oka letter to author, June 9, 1996; Harrington, *Yankee Samurai*, 127, 149, 174, 195, 202, 231.

## 5. The Tatsuguchi Diary

1. Col. Hiromichi Yahara, *The Battle for Okinawa* (New York: John Wiley & Sons, 1995), xii.

2. Herbert Ford (ed.), "Don't Shoot! I Am a Christian!" *Pacific Union College Viewpoint* (Winter, 1981), 4–5, 11–14.

3. Henry K. Yeo (ed.), "Tatsy: Rendezvous at Attu," *Loma Linda University School of Medicine Alumni Journal* (March–April, 1993), 15–16; Gaye LeBaron, "A 'Mystery' Diary Tells a Horror Story of World War II," *Santa Rosa Press Democrat* (October 5, 1992), A2. First Sgt. Charles W. Laird and Pvt. John Hirn each claimed to have found the document that proved to be the Tatsuguchi diary. Sergeant Laird also later claimed that he shot Tatsuguchi.

4. Henry K. Yeo (ed.), "From James Masamichi Niyake," *Loma Linda University School of Medicine Alumni Journal* (March–April, 1993), 22.

5. Yeo, "Tatsy: Rendezvous at Attu," 7.

6. Ibid., 7, 16. Tatsuguchi's premonition of meeting medical school classmates was fulfilled after his death. Joseph Mudry and J.

Lawrence Whitaker both were Seventh Division medical officers. Whitaker, a battalion surgeon, was in the path of the final banzai charge but escaped unharmed. Tatsuguchi was killed not far away.

7. Ford, "Don't Shoot!," 11.

8. Desmond, *Tides of War: World News Reporting,* 252n. The secretary of war awarded Montrose a special citation for his action. Montrose later broke his leg and was hospitalized for a month.

9. G-2 Report no. 67, annex 4, September 4, 1943.

10. Ford, "Don't Shoot!," 13.

## 6. Looking Beyond the Aleutians

1. Otis Hays, Jr., *Home from Siberia: The Secret Odysseys of Interned American Airmen in World War II* (College Station: Texas A&M University Press, 1990), 56.

2. Howard Handleman, *Bridge to Victory* (New York: Random House, 1943) 240; Cloe, *The Aleutian Warriors,* 315.

3. The route from the Aleutians to the Kuriles crossed the international date line; Kurile time is one day ahead of Aleutian time.

4. Hays, *Home from Siberia,* 57–58.

5. Garfield, *The Thousand-Mile War,* 388.

6. Associated Press, International News Service, and United Press retained one correspondent each in Alaska.

7. Harry L. Coles, *The Army Air Forces in World War II,* vol. 4, chap. 11, "The Aleutian Campaign" (Chicago: University of Chicago Press, 1950), 395–96, 400.

8. G-2 Report no. 75, annex 4, October 20, 1943.

9. Alaskan Department Public Proclamation No. 7, November 1, 1943.

## 7. American Prisoners in the Kuriles

1. Hays, *Home from Siberia,* 98.

2. Ibid., 213–23.

3. "Stranger Than Fiction," *Nippon Times* (Tokyo) (undated, 1943). The artwork's caption gave credit to Lieutenant Yokosake for deliberately ramming an American B-24 bomber with his fighter. Both bomber and fighter crashed into the sea. For his sacrifice, Yokosake was posthumously promoted to major.

4. Hays, *Home from Siberia*, 64–67.

5. Albert W. Berecz, MACR no. 2821, RG 92, National Archives.

6. Richard Salter letter to author, December 16, 1995. With fire spreading to a wing of his bomber, Berecz by radio asked Salter what he should do. Salter told him to head for Kamchatka as fast as possible. Days later, Soviet officials told Salter that a life raft with the bodies of the crew had washed up on a Kamchatkan beach. All apparently had died from enemy gunfire.

7. Quinton D. Standiford, MACR no. 2283, RG 92, National Archives.

8. G-2 Report no. 69, September 18, 1943. Radio Tokyo reported that McEowen had revealed that the American raiding mission to Paramushiro had foreseen the possibility of having to make emergency landings in Kamchatka.

9. G-2 Report no. 79, November 27, 1943; Vladimir P. Sabich letter to author, December 27, 1993. Sabich was one of the American airmen interned on Kamchatka following the September 12 raid. As copilot of a nearby B-25 bomber during the Paramushiro attack, he witnessed the destruction of Standiford's bomber: "The entire plane was one big fire ball except for the two wingtips . . . I truly believe that everyone on that plane was completely incinerated before they hit the water."

10. Eleventh Air Force Report of March 10, 1944, attached to MACR no. 2283, RG 92, National Archives.

11. Mary Louise McEowen (widow of Sergeant McEowen) letter to author, June 4, 1994.

12. Takane Ikebe, "Brave Fishermen Capture Yankee Airman in North," *Nippon Times* (Tokyo) (undated, October 1943); "Captive's Confession Bares Fear by Enemy of Japanese," *Nippon Times* (Tokyo) (November 12, 1943).

13. Hays, *Home from Siberia,* 134–35.

14. Albert D. Scott, MACR no. 11271, RG 92, National Archives.

15. Ralph W. Hammond (Head's copilot) letter to author, September 9, 1996. Head and Hammond's B-25 was damaged by enemy fire. Head reported Scott's loss by radio and then crash-landed in Kamchatka.

16. William S. Webb letter to author, October 12, 1996. Webb was Scott's hut mate at the Seventy-seventh Squadron base on Attu. After the war, Webb was reunited with Scott, who related what had happened to him and the crew.

17. Hutchison, *World War II in the North Pacific,* 198.

18. Milton Zack letter to author, May 1, 1990.

19. Lt. Bailey Howard letter to Milton Zack, December 21, 1945. Howard was the Seventy-seventh Squadron's summary court officer on Zack's personal effects after Zack was declared to be missing in action.

20. Walter Bailey letter to author, March 19, 1990.

21. Milton Zack letter to author, May 1, 1990.

22. Richard S. Brevik, MACR no. 14658, RG 92, National Archives.

23. Mitchell Barchuk interview with William Cavanaugh, May 15, 1991.

24. Carl Kulva statement of June 17, 1945, attached to MACR no. 14658, RG 92, National Archives.

25. Barchuk interview with Cavanaugh, May 15, 1991; William Cavanaugh letter to author, October 11, 1991.

## 8. Whither the North Pacific Weather?

1. Alaskan Department Historical Report (undated draft), "Weather," RG 338, National Archives.

2. U.S. Naval Experience in the North Pacific During World War II—Selected Documents (Washington, D.C.: Naval Historical Center, 1989), 78–94.

3. The Aleutian Campaigns, June 1942–August 1943 (Washington, D.C.: Naval Research Center, 1993), 3–4.

4. Eleventh Weather Squadron Historical Report microfilm roll B0017 (Maxwell Air Force Base, Alabama: U.S. Air Force Historical Research Center), frame 1910 (hereafter referred to as Eleventh Weather Squadron History by frame number).

5. Charles C. Bates and John F. Fuller, *America's Weather Warriors* (College Station: Texas A&M University Press, 1986), 112.

6. Eleventh Weather Squadron History, frames 1977–78.

7. Alaskan Department Historical Report, "Weather."

8. Eleventh Weather Squadron History, frames 1910–11.

9. Ibid., frame 1917.

10. Ibid., frames 2918–19.

11. Ibid., frame 1921.

12. Ibid., frames 1929–33.

13. Alaskan Department Historical Report, "Weather."

14. Ibid.

15. A. R. ("Bob") Miller letters to author, September 5 and October 1, 1996.

16. Lee T. Harder, MACR no. 3311, RG 92, National Archives; Eleventh Weather Squadron History, frame 1952.

17. Ralph Wetterhahn, "One Down in Kamchatka," *The Retired Officer Magazine* (January, 2001), 50–56. Fifty-five years later, in November 1999, Russian authorities reported the site of a World War II bomber wreckage in southern Kamchatka between Petropavlovsk and Cape Lopatka near Mutmovsky volcano. A joint U.S.-Russian MIA recovery team identified the wreckage as being that of the Navy PV-1 on which Partier was making his first weather observer flight. The team recovered the remains of the bomber's seven men.

18. Edward P. McDermott, MACR no. 4115, RG 92, National Archives; Eleventh Weather Squadron History, frame 1952.

19. James K. Hastings, MACR no. 14942, RG 92, National Archives.

20. A. R. Miller letter to author, September 5, 1996.

21. Hays, *Home from Siberia*, 214–15.

22. A. R. Miller letter to author, November 7, 1996; Hays, *Home from Siberia*, 178, 183–84.

23. Eleventh Weather Squadron History, frames 2075–78.

24. Ibid., frame 1921.

25. John H. Deane, "Report of the Commanding General, United States Military Mission to Moscow, October 18, 1943–October 31, 1945," RG 334, National Archives, 71–78; G. Patrick March, "Yanks in Siberia (U.S. Navy Weather Stations in the Soviet East Asia, 1945)," *Pacific Historical Review* (August, 1988), 327–42.

## 9. American Deception and Japanese Reaction

1. G-2 Report no. 65, August 21, 1943.

2. G-2 Report no. 72, October 9, 1943.

3. G-2 Report no. 73, October 16, 1943.

4. *Nippon Times* (Tokyo), December 7, 1943.

5. Ibid.

6. G-2 Report no. 79, November 27, 1943.

7. Lt. Gen. Simon B. Buckner, Jr., was the commander of the U.S. Tenth Army against the Japanese forces on Okinawa, where he was killed in action on June 18, 1945.

8. Alaskan Department Public Proclamation No. 10, August 1, 1944.

9. Weinberg, *A World at Arms,* 557–58.

10. Deception Means Against Japan—Alaskan Department, January 1944, RG 165, National Archives; Joint Chiefs of Staff Report of Conference Regarding Plan "Wedlock," August 1, 1944, RG 365, National Archives; Weinberg, *A World at Arms,* 558.

11. G-2 Report no. 97, annex 3, April 1, 1944.

12. G-2 Report no. 98, annex 3, April 6, 1944.

13. G-2 Report no. 100, April 6, 1944.

14. G-2 Report no. 101, annex 3, April 29, 1944.

15. G-2 Reports no. 101, April 29, 1944, and no. 102, May 6, 1944.

16. G-2 Report no. 104, May 20, 1944.

17. G-2 Report no. 104, annex 3, May 20, 1944.

18. G-2 Report no. 105, May 27, 1944.

19. G-2 Report no. 105, annex 3, May 27, 1944.

20. G-2 Report no. 109, June 24, 1944.

21. G-2 Report no. 109, annex 3, June 24, 1944.

22. G-2 Report no. 112, annex 3, July 15, 1944.

23. G-2 Report no. 114, July 29, 1944.

24. G-2 Report no. 114, annex 3, July 29, 1944.

25. G-2 Report no. 115, annex 3, August 5, 1944.

26. G-2 Report no. 116, August 12, 1944.

27. G-2 Report no. 117, August 19, 1944.

28. G-2 Report no. 119, annex 3, September 2, 1944.

29. G-2 Report no. 121, annex 3, September 16, 1944.

30. G-2 Report no. 122, annex 3, September 25, 1944.

31. G-2 Report no. 123, September 30, 1944.

32. G-2 Report no. 124, annex 3, October 7, 1944.

33. G-2 Report no. 125, annex 3, October 14, 1944.

34. G-2 Report no. 126, October 21, 1944.

35. G-2 Report no. 129, November 11, 1944.

36. G-2 Report no. 129, annex 3, November 11, 1944.

37. G-2 Report no. 133, December 9, 1944.

38. G-2 Report no. 131, annex 3, November 25, 1944.

39. G-2 Report no. 162, annex 3, June 30, 1945.

40. G-2 Report no. 166, annex 3, July 28, 1945.

41. Eleventh Air Force Postwar Report, September 11, 1945.

## 10. The Waiting Period in the North Pacific

1. Coles, "The Aleutian Campaign," 394, 396–99, 401.

2. Ibid., 396.

3. Ibid., 400.

4. Charles C. Bradley, *Aleutian Echoes* (Fairbanks: University of Alaska Press, 1994), 35.

5. Ibid., 38–39.

6. Ibid., 53–55.

7. Ibid., 121, 124.

8. Nutchuk (Simeon Oliver), with Alden Hatch, *Back to the Smoky Sea* (New York: Julian Messner, Inc., 1946), 187–90.

9. Bradley, *Aleutian Echoes*, 74.

10. Ibid., 166–86.

11. Robert C. Mikesh, *Japan's World War II Balloon Bomb Attacks on North America* (Washington, D.C.: Smithsonian Institution Press, 1973), 2–17, 25, 27; G-2 Report no. 140, annex 6, January 27, 1945.

12. G-2 Reports no. 140, annex 6, January 27, 1945; no. 144, annex 6, February 17, 1945; no. 146, annex 6, March 10, 1945; no. 147, annex 6, March 17, 1945; and no. 152, annex 6, April 21, 1945.

13. G-2 Report no. 144, annex 6, February 17, 1945.

14. Mikesh, *Japan's World War II Balloon Bomb Attacks*, 38.

15. John J. Stephan, *The Kuril Islands: Russo-Japanese Frontier in the Pacific* (New York: Oxford University Press, 1974), 141–43.

16. Simon Rigge and the Editors of Time-Life Books, *War in the Outposts* (Alexandria, Va.: Time-Life Books, 1980), 144.

17. Gilman, *Our Hidden Front*, 148–49.

18. Alaskan Department Historical Report (undated draft), "Monotony Versus Morale," RG 338, National Archives. Radio Tokyo occasionally used Aleutian items in its foreign propaganda broadcasts, but listenership in the Aleutians was varied among the bored and idle troops. In the beginning, as much as 15 percent of the men listened to and may have believed that some of the propaganda contained factual information. Later, the listener ratio estimates were lowered by half to 8 percent. Because of many other internal factors that influenced fluctuating morale in the Aleutians, Japanese radio propaganda was not a factor of any consequence.

19. G-2 Report no. 59, annex 3, July 11, 1943.

20. G-2 Report no. 66, annex 3, August 28, 1943.

21. G-2 Report no. 71, annex 3, October 2, 1943.

22. Lawrence Reineke letter to author (undated).

23. G-2 Report no. 74, annex 3, October 30, 1943.

24. G-2 Report no. 80, annex 3, December 4, 1943.

25. G-2 Report no. 85, annex 3, January 8, 1944.

26. G-2 Report no. 89, annex 3, February 5, 1944.

27. G-2 Report no. 94, annex 3, March 11, 1944.

28. G-2 Report no. 97, annex 4, April 1, 1944.

29. G-2 Report no. 99, annex 3, April 15, 1944.

30. G-2 Report no. 100, annex 4, April 22, 1944.

31. G-2 Report no. 104, annex 3, May 20, 1944.

32. G-2 Report no. 108, annex 3, June 17, 1944.

33. G-2 Report no. 110, annex 4, July 1, 1944.

34. G-2 Report no. 112, annex 3, July 15, 1944.

35. G-2 Report no. 116, annex 3, August 20, 1944.

36. G-2 Report no. 120, annex 3, September 9, 1944.

37. G-2 Report no. 124, annex 3, October 7, 1944.

38. G-2 Report no. 131, annex 3, November 25, 1944.

39. G-2 Report no. 136, annex 3, December 30, 1944.

40. G-2 Report no. 141, annex 3, February 5, 1945.

41. G-2 Report no. 145, annex 3, March 3, 1945.

42. G-2 Report no. 149, annex 3, March 31, 1945.

43. G-2 Report no. 154, annex 3, May 5, 1945.

44. G-2 Report no. 158, annex 3, June 2, 1945.

45. G-2 Report no. 162, annex 3, June 30, 1945.

46. G-2 Report no. 165, annex 3, July 28, 1945.

47. G-2 Report no. 171, annex 3, September 1, 1945.

## 11. Soviet Presence in the North Pacific

1. Hubert P. van Tuyll, *Feeding the Bear: American Aid to the Soviet Union, 1941–1945* (New York: Greenwood Press, 1989), 26.

2. Rigge, *War in the Outposts,* 76–87.

3. Robert H. Jones, *The Roads to Russia: United States Lend-Lease to the Soviet Union* (Norman: University of Oklahoma Press, 1969), 84–85, 290.

4. Van Tuyll, *Feeding the Bear,* 27.

5. Edward R. Stettinius, Jr., *Lend-Lease, Weapon for Victory* (New York: Macmillan, 1944), 203.

6. Jones, *The Roads to Russia,* 89.

7. Rigge, *War in the Outposts,* 122.

8. George C. Herring, Jr., *Aid to Russia, 1941–1946* (New York: Columbia University Press, 1973), 72.

9. Jones, *The Roads to Russia,* 113, 300.

10. G-2 Report no. 101, April 29, 1944.

11. Stephan, *The Kuril Islands,* 145.

12. John J. Stephan, *The Russian Far East: A History* (Stanford, Calif.: Stanford University Press, 1994), 238–39.

13. Stephan, *The Kuril Islands,* 145.

14. Stephan, *The Russian Far East,* 239; G-2 Report no. 161, annex 3, June 23, 1945. Tokyo domestic radio in a delayed broadcast reported that "the USSR *Transbalt* was sunk by a torpedo at dawn on June 13. Ninety-five members of the crew embarked in five cutters and were left floating on the sea. A Japanese patrol ship spotted and rescued four cutters on June 14 and 15. The aforementioned ship was navigating westward through Soya [La Pérouse] Strait. A Japanese submarine was not operating in that area so, consequently, it is judged that a U.S. submarine was responsible beyond a doubt. The survivors are now in Hokkaido."

15. G-2 Report no. 67, annex 4, September 6, 1943; Jones, *The Roads to Russia,* 272.

16. Jones, *The Roads to Russia,* 209.

17. Ibid., 214; Herring, *Aid to Russia,* 115.

18. Hays, *The Alaska-Siberia Connection,* 12. The vessel had been named in honor of the famous polar aviator who, in 1937, flew nonstop from Moscow to Vancouver, Washington.

19. G-2 Reports no. 64, August 8, 1943, through no. 84, January 1, 1944.

20. Stephan, *The Russian Far East,* 238.

21. Hays, *The Alaska-Siberia Connection,* 26–27.

22. Ibid., 121–22.

23. Jones, *The Roads to Russia,* 290.

24. Ibid., 231.

25. Stan Cohen, *The Forgotten War,* Volume Three (Missoula, Mont.: Pictorial Histories Publishing, 1992), 44–47; Associated Press release (delayed), Cold Bay, Alaska, August 8, 1945.

## 12. Lifting the Security Curtain

1. Koop, *Weapon of Silence,* 132–36.
2. Hays, *The Alaska-Siberia Connection,* 120.
3. Herring, *Aid to Russia,* 183.
4. W. Averill Harriman and Elie Abel, *Special Envoy to Churchill and Stalin, 1941–1946* (New York: Random House, 1975), 400.
5. Stephan, *The Russian Far East,* 240.
6. John Ray Skates, *The Invasion of Japan: Alternative to the Bomb* (Columbia: University of South Carolina Press, 1994), 51–52, 160, 163–64.
7. Ibid., 209–10.
8. Stephan, *The Russian Far East,* 241.
9. Stephan, *The Kuril Islands,* 161.
10. Cohen, *The Forgotten War,* Volume Three, 47.
11. Stephan, *The Russian Far East,* 241–42; Stephan, *The Kuril Islands,* 160–65.
12. John Cloe with Michael Monaghan, *Top Cover for America* (Missoula, Mont.: Pictorial Histories Publishing, 1984), 140.
13. Alaskan Department Public Proclamation No. 11, October 1, 1945.

## Postscript

1. Hays, "When War Came to Seward," 112.
2. Laura Tatsuguchi-Davis letter to author, October 3, 1996; Henry K. Yeo, "About Taeko Tatsuguchi," *Loma Linda University School of Medicine Alumni Journal* (March-April 1993), 21; Ford, "Don't Shoot!," 13–14.
3. Statements made by each ex-prisoner of war to the Commander Submarine Force, U.S. Pacific Fleet, September 12, 1945.

4. Mary Louise McEowen letter to author, June 4, 1994.

5. Hays, *Home from Siberia,* 211–12.

6. Oliver, *Journal of an Aleutian Year,* 249–54.

7. H. S. Yoder, Jr., *Planned Invasion of Japan, 1945: The Siberian Weather Advantage* (Philadelphia: American Philosophical Society, 1997), 6, 112; John R. Deane, *The Strange Alliance* (New York: Viking, 1947), 245; March, "Yanks in Siberia," 327–42.

### Appendix A: Nisei MIS Roster

1. List assembled by author's correspondence with surviving I&I Japanese detachment veterans.

### Appendix B: Propaganda Leaflets

1. Alaska Defense Command G-2 pamphlet, "American Propaganda Leaflets (Aleutian Campaign)," October 25, 1943.

2. Tom Mahoney, "The War of the Leaflets . . . Old and New," *American Legion Magazine* (May, 1966), 8n.

3. G-2 pamphlet, "American Propaganda Leaflets."

### Appendix C: Tatsuguchi Diary Translation

1. Diary translation in author's files; Edward J. Fortier letters to author, June 17 and July 9, 1996. In June 1943, the Alaska Defense Command C-2 ordered Special Agent Edward J. Fortier to confiscate an unauthorized translation of the Tatsuguchi diary from the captain of a fishing schooner en route from the Aleutians to the West Coast.

### Appendix D: Signal Intelligence Operations

1. Ronald H. Spector, *Eagle Against the Sun* (New York: Free Press/Macmillan, 1985), 157, 446–49, 457.

2. Company History of the 131st Signal Service Company, RG 407, National Archives, 3, 7. The original 102nd Signal Radio Intelligence Company was redesignated as the 131st Signal Service Company.

3. Ibid., 1–2.

4. Col. Irving P. Payne letter to author, July 12, 1966; Company History of 131st Signal Service Co., 2. Payne was deputy commander of the company on arrival in Alaska and became company commander.

5. Payne letter to editor, *Alaska Magazine,* January 1988.

6. Alaskan Department Historical Report (undated draft), "The Cottage Operation [Kiska]," RG 338, National Archives, 61, 62.

7. Payne letter to editor, *Alaska Magazine.*

8. G-2 Report no. 60, July 17, 1943.

9. G-2 Report no. 61, July 24, 1943.

10. G-2 Report no. 62, July 31, 1943. Hidden by overcast skies and fogs, a Japanese evacuation fleet successfully reached Kiska on the afternoon of July 28, quickly loaded the entire garrison, and escaped unseen.

11. Alaskan Department Historical Report, "The Cottage Operation," 73–74.

12. G-2 Report no. 63, August 7, 1943.

13. G-2 Report no. 64, August 14, 1943.

14. Company History of 131st Signal Service Co., 5–6.

15. Payne letter to author, September 6, 1996.

# Bibliography

## Books

Bates, Charles C., and John F. Fuller. *America's Weather Warriors.* College Station: Texas A&M University Press, 1986.

Bradley, Charles. *Aleutian Echoes.* Fairbanks: University of Alaska Press, 1994.

Cloe, John H. *The Aleutian Warriors,* Part I. Missoula, Mont.: Pictorial Histories Publishing, 1990.

Cloe, John H., with Michael F. Monaghan. *Top Cover for America.* Missoula, Mont.: Pictorial Histories Publishing, 1984.

Cohen, Stan. *The Forgotten War,* Volume Two. Missoula, Mont.: Pictorial Histories Publishing, 1988.

————. *The Forgotten War,* Volume Three. Missoula, Mont.: Pictorial Histories Publishing, 1992.

Coles, Harry L. *The Army Air Forces in World War II,* vol. 6, chap. 11. "The Aleutian Campaign." Chicago: University of Chicago Press, 1950.

Crost, Lyn. *Honor by Fire: Japanese Americans at War in Europe and the Pacific.* Novato, Calif.: Presidio Press, 1994.

Deane, John R. *The Strange Alliance.* New York: Viking, 1947.

Desmond, Robert W. *Tides of War: World News Reporting, 1931–1945.* Iowa City: University of Iowa Press, 1984.

Garfield, Brian. *The Thousand-Mile War.* Fairbanks: University of Alaska Press, 1995.

Gilman, William. *Our Hidden Front.* New York: Reynal & Hitchcock, 1944.

Goldstein, Donald M., and Katherine V. Dillon (eds.),. *Fading Victory: The Diary of Admiral Matome Ugaki, 1941–1945.* Pittsburgh: University of Pittsburgh Press, 1991.

————. *The Williwaw War.* Fayetteville: University of Arkansas Press, 1992.

Handleman, Howard. *Bridge to Victory.* New York: Random House, 1943.

Harriman, W. Averell, and Elie Abel. *Special Envoy to Churchill and Stalin, 1941–1946.* New York: Random House, 1975.

Harrington, Joseph D. *Yankee Samurai: The Secret Role of Nisei in America's Pacific Victory.* Detroit: Pettigrew Enterprises, 1979.

Hashimoto, Mochitsura. *Sunk! The Story of the Japanese Submarine Fleet, 1941–1945.* New York: Henry Holt and Company, 1954.

Hays, Otis, Jr. *The Alaska-Siberia Connection: The World War II Air Route.* College Station: Texas A&M University Press, 1996.

————. *Home from Siberia: The Secret Odysseys of Interned American Airmen in World War II.* College Station: Texas A&M University Press, 1990.

Herring, George C., Jr. *Aid to Russia, 1941–1946.* New York: Columbia University Press, 1973.

Hutchison, Kevin Don. *World War II in the North Pacific.* Westport, Conn.: Greenwood Press, 1994.

Jones, Robert H. *The Roads to Russia: United States Lend-Lease to the Soviet Union.* Norman: University of Oklahoma Press, 1969.

Kohlhoff, Dean. *When the Wind Was a River: Aleut Evacuation in World War II.* Seattle: University of Washington Press, 1995.

Koop, Theodore F. *Weapon of Silence.* Chicago: University of Chicago Press, 1946.

Mikesh, Robert C. *Japan's World War II Balloon Bomb Attacks on North America.* Washington, D.C.: Smithsonian Institution Press, 1973.

Mott, Frank Luther. *American Journalism.* New York: Macmillan, 1950.

Nutchuk (Simeon Oliver), with Alden Hatch. *Back to the Smoky Sea.* New York: Julian Messner, Inc., 1946.

Oliver, Ethel Ross. *Journal of an Aleutian Year.* Seattle: University of Washington Press, 1998.

Prados, John. *Combined Fleet Decoded: The Secret History of American Intelligence and the Japanese Navy in World War II.* New York: Random House, 1995.

Rigge, Simon, and the Editors of Time-Life Books. *War in the Outposts.* Alexandria, Va.: Time-Life Books, 1980.

Rourke, Norman E. *War Comes to Alaska: The Dutch Harbor Attack, June 3–4, 1942.* Shippensburg, Pa.: White Mane Publishing Co., 1997.

Skates, John Ray. *The Invasion of Japan: Alternative to the Bomb.* Columbia: University of South Carolina Press, 1994.

Spector, Ronald H. *Eagle Against the Sun.* New York: Free Press/Macmillan, 1985.

Stephan, John J. *The Kuril Islands: Russo-Japanese Frontier in the Pacific.* New York: Oxford University Press, 1974.

————. *The Russian Far East: A History.* Stanford, Calif.: Stanford University Press, 1994.

Stettinius, Edward R., Jr. *Lend-Lease, Weapon for Victory.* New York: Macmillan, 1944.

Van Tuyll, Herbert P. *Feeding the Bear: American Aid to the Soviet Union, 1941–1945.* New York: Greenwood Press, 1989.

Weinberg, Gerhard L. *A World at Arms.* New York: Cambridge University Press, 1994.

Yahara, Col. Hiromichi. *The Battle for Okinawa.* New York: John Wiley & Sons, 1995.

Yoder, H. S., Jr. *Planned Invasion of Japan, 1945: The Siberian Weather Advantage.* Philadelphia: American Philosophical Society, 1997.

## Articles

"Attu Island Is Blasted Under Shower of Japanese Bombs." *Nippon Times* (Tokyo) (December 7, 1943).

"Brave Fishermen Capture Yankee Airman in North." *Nippon Times* (Tokyo) (undated October, 1943).

"Captive's Confession Bares Fear by Enemy of Japanese." *Nippon Times* (Tokyo) (November 12, 1943).

Ford, Herbert (ed.). "Don't Shoot! I Am a Christian!" *Pacific Union College Viewpoint* (Winter, 1981).

Hays, Otis, Jr. "The Silent Years in Alaska." *Alaska Journal* (1986 anthology).

————. "When War Came to Seward." *Alaska Journal* (Autumn, 1983).

Inouye, Ronald K. "Harry Sotaro Kawabe: Issei Businessman of Seward and Seattle." *Alaska History* (Spring, 1990).

LeBaron, Gaye. "A 'Mystery' Diary Tells a Horror Story of World War II." *Santa Rosa Press Democrat* (October 25, 1992).

Mahoney, Tom. "The War of the Leaflets . . . Old and New." *American Legion Magazine* (May, 1966).

March, G. Patrick. "Yanks in Siberia (U.S. Navy Weather Stations in Soviet Asia, 1945)." *Pacific Historical Review* (August, 1988).

Watterhahn, Ralph. "One Down in Kamchatka." *The Retired Officer Magazine* (January, 2001).

Yeo, Henry K. (ed.). "About Taeko Tatsuguchi." *Loma Linda University School of Medicine Alumni Journal* (March–April, 1993).

————. "From James Masamichi Miyake." *Loma Linda University School of Medicine Alumni Journal* (March–April, 1993).

————. "Tatsy: Rendezvous at Attu." *Loma Linda University School of Medicine Alumni Journal* (March–April, 1993).

## Documents

Alaska Defense Command/Alaskan Department G-2 Weekly Periodic Reports, together with annex no. 3 (Psychological), annex no. 4 (Counterintelligence), annex no. 6 (Air Information), 1943–1945, Record Group 338, National Archives.

Alaska Defense Command G-2 pamphlet. "American Propaganda Leaflets (Aleutian Campaign)," 1943. Author's files.

———. "Emergency Foods in the Aleutians," 1943. Author's files.

Alaska Defense Command Public Proclamation No. 1, April 7, 1942. Author's files.

Alaska Defense Command Public Proclamation No. 4, June 30, 1942. Author's files.

Alaskan Department Historical Report (undated draft). "The Cottage Operation [Kiska]." Record Group 338, National Archives.

———. "Monotony Versus Morale." Record Group 338, National Archives.

———. "Weather." Record Group 338, National Archives.

Alaskan Department Public Proclamation No. 7, November 1, 1943. Author's files.

Alaskan Department Public Proclamation No. 10, August 1, 1944. Author's files.

Alaskan Department Public Proclamation No. 11, October 1, 1945. Author's files.

The Aleutians Campaign, June 1942–August 1943. Naval Historical Center, Washington, D.C., 1993.

Company History of the 131st Signal Service Company (undated). Record Group 407, National Archives.

Deane, John R. "Report of the Commanding General, United States Mission to Moscow, October 18, 1943–October 31, 1945." Record Group 334, National Archives.

Deception Means Against Japan—Alaskan Department, January 1944. Record Group 165, National Archives.

DeWitt, Lt. Gen. John L. Letter to Alaska Territorial Gov. Ernest Gruening, August 6, 1941. Author's files.

Eleventh Air Force Missing Air Crew Reports (MACR) nos. 2283, 2821, 3311, 4115, 11271, 14658, and 14942. Record Group 92, National Archives.

Eleventh Weather Squadron Historical Report, January 1941–July 1944. Film roll B0017, Call no. SQ-WEA-HI. U.S. Air Force Historical Research Center, Maxwell Air Force Base, Alabama.

Joint Chiefs of Staff Report of Conference Regarding Plan "Wedlock," August 1944. Record Group 365, National Archives.

U.S. Naval Experience in the North Pacific During World War II—Selected Documents. Naval Historical Center, Washington, D.C., 1989.

# Index

Note: Italicized page numbers refer to figures.